T0330770

ROUTLEDGE LIBRARY EDITIONS:
SOVIET ECONOMICS

Volume 1

AGRICULTURAL CO-OPERATION IN THE SOVIET UNION

AGRICULTURAL CO-OPERATION IN THE SOVIET UNION

G. RATNER

Edited by
THE HORACE PLUNKETT
FOUNDATION

Translator:
M. DIGBY

Routledge
Taylor & Francis Group

LONDON AND NEW YORK

First published in 1929 by George Routledge & Sons, Ltd.

This edition first published in 2023
by Routledge
4 Park Square, Milton Park, Abingdon, Oxon OX14 4RN

and by Routledge
605 Third Avenue, New York, NY 10158

Routledge is an imprint of the Taylor & Francis Group, an informa business

© 1929

All rights reserved. No part of this book may be reprinted or reproduced or utilised in any form or by any electronic, mechanical, or other means, now known or hereafter invented, including photocopying and recording, or in any information storage or retrieval system, without permission in writing from the publishers.

Trademark notice: Product or corporate names may be trademarks or registered trademarks, and are used only for identification and explanation without intent to infringe.

British Library Cataloguing in Publication Data
A catalogue record for this book is available from the British Library

ISBN: 978-1-032-48466-2 (Set)
ISBN: 978-1-032-49009-0 (Volume 1) (hbk)
ISBN: 978-1-032-49012-0 (Volume 1) (pbk)
ISBN: 978-1-003-39181-4 (Volume 1) (ebk)

DOI: 10.4324/9781003391814

Publisher's Note
The publisher has gone to great lengths to ensure the quality of this reprint but points out that some imperfections in the original copies may be apparent.

Disclaimer
The publisher has made every effort to trace copyright holders and would welcome correspondence from those they have been unable to trace.

AGRICULTURAL CO-OPERATION IN THE SOVIET UNION

First edition March, 1929

Agricultural Co-operation in the Soviet Union

By

G. Ratner

Edited by

The Horace Plunkett Foundation

Translator : M. Digby

LONDON

GEORGE ROUTLEDGE & SONS, LTD.

BROADWAY HOUSE : 68–74 CARTER LANE, E.C.

1929

ERRATA

Page 19, line 6, *for* 4,250,000 *read* 4,250,000,000.
Page 62, line 2 from the bottom, *for* millions *read* milliards.

PRINTED IN GREAT BRITAIN BY
BILLING AND SONS LTD., GUILDFORD AND ESHER

CONTENTS

CONTENTS

EDITORIAL

THE survival of co-operation in Russia is in itself para-
doxical to those who see antithesis in the voluntary
character of the one and the authoritarian socialism of
the other; its promotion and expansion under a State
Communist régime is a phenomenon that cries for
documentation. If the rulers of Russia, with a
theoretical prejudice as strong as that of any capitalist
against an autonomous form of non-profit-making
business association, have found agricultural co-operation essential to the redemption and progress of Russian
agriculture, the significance of it, to those concerned
with economic problems of rural life, transcends that
of all other experiments pursued in the social laboratory
of the Revolution, and not least of all to those com-
munities within the British Empire which tend to
throw upon the state the responsibility for a solution
of their agricultural business problems.

That this, in fact, has been the persuasion and
practice of the Russian Government since 1921,
emerges from the cumulative evidence of this survey,
more convincing than any legislation or other declara-
tions of policy, though in these also the tendency was
manifest. Since that date the formation of voluntary
autonomous societies among farmers and small-holders
has not only been permitted, as in England, but
encouraged. Before the war there were 22,000 such
societies in what is now the territory of the Union of
Soviet Socialist Republics; many of them were swept

away by the violence of war and revolution. War and revolution, moreover, brought with them an ideology which, though not hostile to the aims of co-operation, held that they might be more logically and expeditiously fulfilled if what had been a voluntary business movement became completely integrated with the machinery of the Socialist state. The business of many co-operative societies and their unions was taken over by organisations entirely controlled by local Soviets and the Government. But this proved no more than a phase, and at the end of the Civil War in 1921 the new economic policy of the Soviet Government was established with the promotion of all forms of co-operation, especially amongst the peasants, as one of its essential features. In 1921 there survived only about half of the original number of voluntary societies with an unbroken tradition upon which to build a new movement. In other words, the destructive effects of war and revolution upon the Russian movement were approximately the same as that which the Irish movement suffered, and not worse than the movement experienced under the rule of Fascism in Italy; though in Italy also, where for years all one could learn about the organisations was that they were being disintegrated and immobilised by the intrigues and " prepotenze " of Fascism, co-operation is again coming into its own, to judge by the National Exhibition held last year in Rome. Be that as it may, the surprising fact of comparison between the fate of agricultural co-operation in these three countries is that neither under Fascism nor under the exemplary policy of the Irish Free State has a revival of the movement taken place in the proportions of that of Russia, which in seven years can show an increase of autonomous societies from about 12,000 to 100,000 and back up these figures with a corresponding increase in the volume of co-operative business.

Now the point which, for our purpose, this volume is intended to drive home, requires little sharpening. The Russian Government, with its principle of reconstructing all national economic life and enterprise on a state socialist basis, and the power to do so, found this principle inapplicable to the primary organisation of agricultural business; even in the larger collective and transport stages of marketing it has permitted and encouraged the operation of voluntary and autonomous federations of societies. State farming also has been tried and is still being carried on, but the part played by these State farms is inconsiderable. They may be compared with the so-called " co-operative farms " of our English societies, and seem no more likely to indicate a true solution of the agricultural problems of today. Yet never could a government have had greater incentive to make a success of state farming; never was a situation more ripe for compulsory marketing of farm produce under state management.

There is no magic, it is often said, in co-operation; it has not brought prosperity to Russia's rural millions at a touch of the wand. But this at least the Russian peasant knows—as a member of his co-operative society he has an equal voice with his fellows in the control of his own business organisation reaching past all frontiers to his markets, through which also he obtains in full the value of his produce without toll of profit for capitalist or state.

Is there not something peculiar, then, if not magical, in a form of association developed in many lands in

EDITORIAL

spite of a predatory capitalism, even in the most capitalistic United States, and surviving here in spite of an all-absorbing Communism, finally to be chosen as the rural economic basis of the Union of Socialist Soviet Republics ?

K. W.

10, DOUGHTY STREET,
LONDON, W.C. 1.
December, 1928.

PREFACE

In spite of the large scope of the activities of the agricultural co-operatives of the U.S.S.R. and the quick response of the peasant population, this movement still remains unknown to the co-operators and business people of Western Europe and America. There is no printed matter illuminating the subject, with the exception of a few articles appearing in periodicals. At the same time over a thousand commercial and industrial firms, as well as a number of banks and co-operative organisations, have already established business relations with the agricultural co-operative organisations of the U.S.S.R., frequently granting them large credits and coming into constant contact with them.

We consider that the interest amongst business circles and the demand for a pamphlet containing the description of the activities of the agricultural co-operatives in the U.S.S.R. make the publication of such a pamphlet advisable.

This pamphlet does not give a detailed analysis of the co-operative movement in general, but limits itself to a description of the actual work of the agricultural co-operatives.

The interest which was aroused by the publication of this pamphlet in German (published in Berlin in October, 1928, by Paul Parey) induces the author to have it published in English.

The rapid growth of co-operation and the develop-

PREFACE

ment of its various forms make necessary a frequent revision of its literature. The present work is supplemented by statistical data and recent facts not to be found in the German edition.

The author of this book, realising its unavoidable defects, will be very grateful to all readers and especially to English co-operators who will point out these defects to him.

G. RATNER,

Member of the Board of the Union of
Agricultural Co-operative Unions.

Moscow,
   B. DMITROWKA 4,
     December 28, 1928.

AGRICULTURAL CO-OPERATION IN THE SOVIET UNION

I. THE PRESENT POSITION OF AGRICULTURAL CO-OPERATION

THE history of agricultural co-operation in the U.S.S.R. begins after the close of the civil war when the Soviet government could turn its hand to the reconstruction of its shattered national economy, and especially of its agriculture.

Formal foundations for the rebuilding of agricultural co-operation were laid at the introduction of the New Economic Policy (N.E.P.). This was effected by an order of the Council of the People's Commissars of 17th May, 1921, confirmed by the All-Russian Central Executive Committee on the 16th August of the same year.

In the then existing conditions of falling currency and a system of collecting agricultural taxes by means of levy in kind, these formal foundations alone were insufficient to give agricultural co-operation a fresh start. But after thorough financial reform, a restoration of the currency, and the adoption of practical measures for the reconstruction and development of national economy as a whole, there set in a rapid growth of the co-operative movement, which has since expanded into a powerful organisation.

In the U.S.S.R. the agricultural co-operatives stand, in relation to the general economic interests of individual peasant economy, as the final goal in the organisation of agriculture on a socialist basis.

B

AGRICULTURAL CO-OPERATION

Agricultural co-operation now exists for the following fundamental purposes:

(a) Organisation of the processing and sale of agricultural products.

(b) Supply to the peasants of the requirements of production and consumption.

(c) Organisation of co-operative credit.

(d) Improvement of the technical side of peasant economy.

(e) Development of forms of collective agriculture.

In the first years of its existence, when the market output of the peasants was still small, agricultural co-operation developed along the lines of an agricultural general purposes movement, through whose agency the members disposed of their produce and obtained what manufactured articles they required. Through these general purposes co-operatives the peasants also obtained credit.

With the restoration of different branches of agriculture, particularly in those districts where special crops were produced, there appeared, as output increased, a tendency toward specialisation among the primary co-operative societies. This development took place with peculiar rapidity in those branches of agriculture whose products undergo processing before reaching the market. Thus in the dairying areas (West Siberia and Ural) there arose butter-makers' co-operative societies which grew rapidly; in the potato districts (Kostroma, Jaroslav, etc.) there appeared special co-operative societies for processing potatoes, the manufacture of treacle, starch, potato flour, etc.

In districts such as Turkmanistan and Usbekistan, special cotton co-operative societies have been formed to organise the sowing of fields for cotton growing, and transmit the surplus product to the state factories.

2

In the Black Earth District of the R.S.F.S.R. and in the Ukraine, special beet-sugar manufacturing societies have been formed. In the Crimean Republic and in the Transcaucasian Federation—particularly in Abkhazia—special co-operative unions of tobacco and wine growers and market gardeners have been organised.

Special seed and pedigree stock-breeding co-operatives have been established for the encouragement of plant and animal culture. Still further special co-operatives have been formed for the ownership of machinery and tractors, for land improvement, and so on. Beside these forms of the co-operative movement which unite individual peasants for joint sale, supply or production, there have arisen co-operatives which introduce a collective labour system, to the exclusion of individual husbandry. Such are the complicated forms of co-operative association for the joint cultivation of the soil and the agricultural communes and artels.

Contemporaneous with the formation of special co-operatives undertaking the supply of requirements to their members, the disposal of agricultural produce or the collective organisation of labour processes, there took place a popular movement towards the organisation of co-operative credit. For this purpose agricultural credit societies were formed.

The co-operative movement of the U.S.S.R. must be studied, according to the functions it has to fulfil, in some fifty different forms. This multiplicity of the co-operative type is closely related to the varied character of individual districts and regions as well as to the different agricultural processes.

3

AGRICULTURAL CO-OPERATION

POSITION OF ORGANISED AGRICULTURAL CO-OPERATION

The returns of the Central Statistical Board and of the Central agricultural co-operative organisations give the following picture of the development of individual local societies—so-called " primary co-operatives "—in the U.S.S.R.:

Year.	Number of Co-operatives.	Increase Since 1920.	Increase Since the Previous Year.
		Per Cent.	Per Cent.
1920 ..	12,850	100	—
1921 ..	24,060	187	187
1922 ..	22,261	171	92
1923 ..	31,187	243	142
1924 ..	37,872	295	122
October 1, 1925 ..	54,813	427	145
October 1, 1926 ..	66,037	520	122
October 1, 1927 ..	79,340	614	118
April 1, 1928 ..	93,400[1]	727	145

Thus every year has witnessed a territorial extension of the network of agricultural co-operatives, a growth which greatly exceeds that of agricultural co-operation in the pre-war period. The number of co-operatives increased particularly in 1927-28, when there was a mass organisation of small productive agricultural societies (such as societies for common use of agricultural machinery and cultivation of land). Before the war there were only 27,000 agricultural co-operatives in the territories of the former Russian Empire, which, after deducting those districts which do not today form part

[1] So-called "wild" co-operatives which are not members of a union or of the great agricultural credit societies are not included in the figures for April 1, 1928, as there is no exact data to hand. Together with the "wilds" the number of the co-operatives reaches 100,000, embracing about 12·5 million members.

4

of the U.S.S.R. (Poland, Lithuania, Finland, etc.), leaves about 22,000 societies. Today there are 100,000 (" wild "included)—something like five times as many.

Progress in the co-operative transformation of peasant economy is illustrated by the following figures:

	Oct. 1, 1923.	Oct. 1, 1924.	Oct. 1, 1925.	Oct. 1, 1926.	Oct. 1, 1927.	April 1, 1928.
Number of members in millions[1]	1·20	2·77	5·73	7·88	10·09	11·3
Per cent. of growth ..	100	231	478	663	847	941
Per cent. since previous year	—	231	207	139	127	120

It is evident from the above figures that from October 1, 1927, to April 1, 1928, the number of co-operatives increased very rapidly (45 per cent.), whereas the increase in membership is considerably smaller (20 per cent.). This is explained by the fact that during this period there was a mass organisation in agriculture of co-operatives for collective farming and for other simple productive purposes (see page 57), consisting of a small number of peasant families—e.g., one Association (Artel) consists on an average of 20 families and one Credit Association of 726 families. With regard to the agricultural credit and special marketing co-operatives, these show an equal increase in number, whereas the number of farms embraced by co-operation increases more rapidly than the number of co-operatives. The number of members of the credit co-operatives increased by 25·3 per cent. and the

[1] In these figures the " wild " co-operative societies are included. On October 1, 1926, these societies stood at 21 per cent., and on October 1, 1927, at 18·6 per cent. of the total. On October 1, 1926, they included 14·8 per cent., and on October 1, 1927, 6 per cent. of the total membership of al! co-operative societies.

5

number of the co-operatives increased only by 9 per cent., which proves that the co-operatives have become larger.

The large increase in the number of productive societies (simple productive societies and collective farms) is explained by the active co-operative propaganda, as well as by easy credit terms and the granting of subsidies for production. At the same time it points to the fact that the advantages of the use of agricultural machinery are beginning to be appreciated by the peasants, creating in them a strong tendency to the unification of their agricultural activities. Newly formed productive societies mostly become members of the large local credit co-operatives and not of the Unions.

The peasant households brought within the movement by April 1, 1928, amount to 50 per cent. of the total number of peasant households in the U.S.S.R., taking the number of households connected with the co-operative movement ("wild" societies included) as 12·5 millions, and the total number of peasant households as 25 millions (as given in the returns of the Central Statistical Board). It must be observed here that there are cases in which peasants are simultaneously members of two societies (for instance, a creamery and a credit society), and thus appear twice in the statistics. We assume that such cases amount to 20 per cent. of total membership.

The primary co-operatives, that is the individual societies, are united in co-operative unions or secondary societies. In the first years of its existence Soviet co-operation formed itself almost exclusively into general purposes unions, which included co-operatives of every type amongst their members. With the development of special local societies there began also the specialisation of the secondary type of co-operative, the unions. Thus, simultaneously with the growth of general purposes unions, were created special unions for butter production, potato processing, cattle breeding, grain marketing, etc. These unions again may be divided into two kinds, those which only unite special societies (for instance, milk or tobacco co-operatives), and those which include amongst their members both general purposes societies and various special societies. The latter are only bound to the union in respect of certain commodities.

In a number of regions the secondary unions organise themselves through their regional, national or economic affinities into tertiary unions, which take a region or a republic as their sphere of operations.

With the introduction in 1928 of large territorial economic units (" economic regions ") with corresponding regional administrations (Lower Volga Region, with Saratov as centre, Middle Volga Region, with Samara as centre, Central Black Earth Region—Voronesh) the organisation of regional unions (" tertiary unions ") for special products had been introduced.

The agricultural credit societies have been the subject of special developments. On the one hand, they are linked up with the agricultural co-operative unions, for whom they undertake the disposal of agricultural produce and the purchase of agricultural requirements; on the other hand, they are bound to the state credit institutions, who act as agents for the transmission of state credit assigned to agriculture, particularly co-operative credit. Now, however, the co-operative unions are gradually taking over the provision of credit to their members, and are thus replacing the state crcdit organisations. The central institution of agricultural credit is the " Central Agricultural Bank," which, though it represents a state institution, is strongly influenced by the agricultural co-operatives.

In the first years of the New Economic Policy (N.E.P.),

introduced in 1921, the local unions of the agricultural co-operative movement of the Soviet Union (excepting the Ukraine) united in the Central Union " Selskosojus " (All-Russian Union of Agricultural Co-operatives), which was carrying out both organising and trading functions. With the development of special branches and regions of agriculture and the simultaneous establishment of special co-operative societies and unions, special central unions of agricultural co-operation began to be evolved from the Selskosojus.

Now there are in the R.S.F.S.R. sixteen such special central unions, established at different times and each occupied with a special branch of work. The first Central Union, which separated itself from the Selskosojus in 1922, is the " Sojus Kartoffel," the central union of potato growers co-operatives. After it came the " Lnocentr," a central union which undertook to dispose of the flax and hemp output of the general purposes societies, supplied the flax and hemp industries with the raw materials of production, and organised the mechanical processing of flax and hemp. In the years that followed there were formed out of the Selskosojus:

The Central Union of Milk and Creamery Co-operatives, " Maslocentr," *i.e.*, Buttercentre.

The Central Union of Fruit and Vegetable Growers and Wine Producers Co-operatives, " Plodovinsojus."

The Central Union of Tobacco Growers Co-operatives, " Centrotabaksojus."

The Central Union of Eggs and Poultry Co-operative Societies, " Ptizevodsojus."

The Central Union of Grain Growers Co-operative Societies, " Khlebocentr."

The Central Union of Animal and Livestock Products Co-operative Societies, " Zhivotnovodsojus."

8

IN THE SOVIET UNION

The Central Union of Bee-keepers Co-operatives, " Pchelovodsojus."

The Central Union of Seed Growers Co-operatives, " Semenovodosjus."

The Central Union of Sugar-Beet Co-operatives, " Sveklocentr."

Further, a Union was formed to unite the collective farming organisations called " Kolchoscentr." The Central Union of the Forestry Co-operatives, which was formerly affiliated to the Agricultural Co-operative Central organisation, " Vsekoles," in July, 1928, affiliated itself to the group of industrial co-operatives.

In addition to the special Central Unions thus formed by a federation of unions and co-operatives organised for the special departments of agriculture, there remain to be mentioned certain central unions which serve the whole system of agricultural co-operation. These are The Central Union of Co-operative Insurance Societies, " Koopstrachsojus "; The Central Union for publishing and for supplying all agricultural co-operatives with book-keeping and accountancy requirements, stationery, books, wireless sets, etc., " Knigosojus "; and, lastly, The Central Co-operative Bank, which serves all kinds of co-operatives (including the consumers and industrial productive societies), the " Vsekobank."

In the Ukrainian Soviet Republic there is an independent central organisation, " Silski Gospodar," and four departmental central unions: " Kooptach," the central union for egg and poultry co-operatives; " Burak Spilka," the central union of sugar-beet co-operatives; " Dobrobut," the central union of dairying and live-stock products co-operatives; and " Plodospilka," the central union of fruit and vegetable co-operatives.

In other independent republics (Transcaucasian,

White-Russia, Turkmanistan and Uzbek) there are central unions which are affiliated to the "Council of the Union of Unions" (see below). The agricultural co-operatives of each independent republic are quite independent in their activities.

The individual central unions, the republican unions of autonomous republics, as well as the most important local unions of the R.S.F.S.R., are once more federated in one leading organisation at the head of the whole agricultural co-operation of R.S.F.S.R.—"The Union of Unions of Agricultural Co-operation" ("Sojus Sojusov"), which is the leading organ of all the central as well as local agricultural co-operative organisations of the R.S.F.S.R.

The Union of Unions carries on no trading activities and works as a central organ of the agricultural co-operative system in the R.S.F.S.R., concerned with leadership but not with commercial business. Its task is to achieve, both in the work of organisation and in the economic activity of all central organisations and all types of agricultural co-operation, a common, co-ordinated participation and influence in the decision of all questions which concern the whole system of agricultural co-operation, to act as its representative and to keep in practical and scientific touch with the general agricultural co-operative movement. The agricultural co-operatives of all the republics in the U.S.S.R. are quite independent in their activities. From time to time a Council of the agricultural co-operatives of the U.S.S.R. is called for the purpose of discussing the question of united work and mutual representation, and in order to talk over the question of the co-operative movement in principle. This Council has a permanent Board comprising the leaders of the agricultural co-operatives of the republican Unions. This Board was first elected in December, 1928.

But this does not conclude the organisation of agricultural co-operation in the U.S.S.R. Not all agricultural co-operatives are members of the agricultural co-operative organisation. Out of 79,340 co-operatives, with a membership of 10 million peasant households, 14,000 co-operatives, with a membership of 620,000 peasant households, remained on October 1, 1927, outside the co-operative system. These are known as " wild " co-operative societies. These are small special societies, the majority for supply of machinery and improvement of stock-breeding. The problem of bringing these societies into the unions is a difficult one, as a method has to be found by which these small, weak co-operatives are not affiliated direct to the unions, but are attached to a strong neighbouring agricultural credit society. The rules of credit societies allow them to accept as members not only individual peasants but small peasants' groups of various kinds.

All unions are without exception affiliated to the Central Unions. The progressive growth, in particular of the special unions, can be seen from the following table:

	General Purpose Unions.	Special Unions.	Total.	Percentage of Special Unions to Total.
				Per Cent.
October 1, 1925 ..	326	77	403	18·9
October 1, 1926 ..	285	108	393	28·5
October 1, 1927 ..	264	147	411	36·0
April 1, 1928 ..	255	176	431	40·8
October 1, 1928 ..	255	260	515	50·5

The organisation of agricultural co-operation in the U.S.S.R. as described above may be represented by the diagram on page 13.

Diagram of the Organisation of Agricultural Co-operation in the R.S.F.S.R.

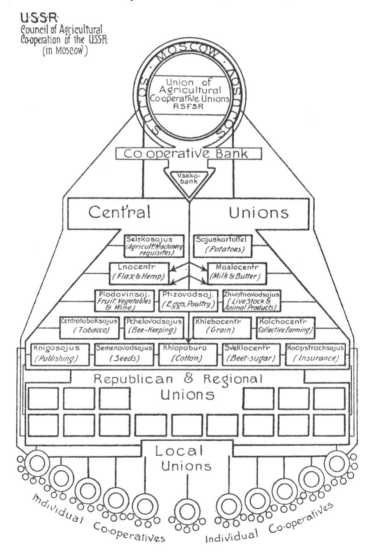

U·S·S·R·
Council of Agricultural
Co-operation of the USSR·
(in Moscow)

II. THE LEGAL FOUNDATIONS OF AGRICULTURAL CO-OPERATION

The primary co-operative societies, like those of higher grade—the Unions and Central organisations—were formed by voluntary association of their members. Article 49 of the law on agricultural co-operation runs:

" The agricultural co-operative organisations are formed at the free will of the persons and organisations interested therein, and the adhesion of new members takes place in the same way."

All citizens enjoying full civil rights, who are occupied in agriculture and are bound to it professionally, may become members of an agricultural co-operative; legal entities may also become members so long as they are established in the district in question and are co-operatively organised; this includes public utility societies which undertake agriculture. Co-operatives of any kind can be members of an agricultural credit society, provided their headquarters is in the same district as that of the credit society.

The law provides that the number of founders of an agricultural co-operative society shall not be less than 10 persons, and of an agricultural credit society, 50 persons. Without in any way hindering the peasants from uniting in co-operative organisations of any form which meets with their wishes and needs, the law requires a certain basic type of rules, together with statements on the following points:

(1) Name of the organisation. (2) Sphere of operations and place of office. (3) General aim of the organisation and concrete objects of activity addressed to that aim. (4) Stipulations with regard to entrance,

resignation and exclusion of members. (5) Form and method of formation of capital. (6) Value of shares, entrance fees and other compulsory contributions, if such are envisaged. (7) Liability of members to the organisation. (8) Method of distributing the net profit or loss. (9) Stipulation of the requirements for the dissolution of the organisation and methods of liquidation.

The law devotes special attention to the formation of capital, both share-capital and reserve. The liability of the member to the society is also specially considered. It is also provided in the legal stipulations that agricultural co-operative societies should be liable with all their resources for all obligations they have entered into. For this purpose the agricultural and agricultural credit co-operatives must lay down by rule the subsequent liability of their members in cases where the resources of a society do not cover its obligations and the society is dissolved. The subsequent liability of the member is limited to a stipulated multiple of his shares, or of the credit opened in his name. In practice, the liability of the co-operative member is fixed at ten times the amount of his share-holding. Each new member, however, is liable for the obligations incurred by the society prior to his entrance.

The business of agricultural co-operatives is carried on on the principle of free self-government. The law provides that all members have equal rights—that is, that the holders of several shares receive no preferential treatment either in the business management of the organisation or the distribution of profit.

A general meeting of members or their proxies elects, as governing body, a board which must consist of members of the society itself, An auditing commission acts as controlling body. Further, a supervisory council may be elected at the wish of the general meeting. The election of a supervisory council in addition to an auditing commission is compulsory in the case of agricultural credit societies and unions.

The entrance of primary societies into higher unions is controlled by statutory provisions. The law knows no limitations to such an entrance. Article 45 of the legal provisions runs:

" Agricultural co-operative unions are formed for the support of their members in the fulfilment of their co-operative and economic duties."

For agricultural credit unions, the law lays down that, besides agricultural credit societies, other types of co-operative organisation, acting in an agricultural sphere, may be accepted as members. It is, however, an indispensable condition that the majority of co-operatively organised persons who are represented in a credit union should be members of the agricultural credit societies of the union in question. In other respects the same rules apply to unions as to primary societies.

The same legal provisions are applicable to the foundation of central co-operative unions. The possibility of a union joining a central union is solely and exclusively determined by the rules of the central union. These rules also fix the formation of the original capital, the amount of shares and subsequent contributions, and the proportion of profits to be carried over to capital. The liability of the central unions for their obligations is precisely the same as in the case of the subordinate organisations. Here also the unions affiliated to the central organisation are liable for a fixed multiple of their shareholding or the credit advanced to them.

III. COMMERCIAL ACTIVITY OF THE
AGRICULTURAL CO-OPERATIVES

The agricultural co-operative unites the peasants for productive purposes, for the disposal of their agricultural produce, as well as for the supply of the manufactured goods and products which they require for their productive activities. The peasants are supplied with articles of consumption by the consumers' co-operative. The sale of products of home industries (so-called " Kustar " home industries) takes place through special " Kustar " co-operatives, whose head organisation is the " Vsekopromsojus."

Consequently the total turnover of the agricultural co-operatives falls into two sections of sale and supply. The following figures, in million roubles,[1] give a comprehensive picture of the extent of the turnover in supply and sale of the *local co-operatives*:

	Supply.	Sale.	Total.	Percentage.
1923/24	166	212	378	100
1924/25	332	369	701	185
1925/26	442	691	1,133	300
1926/27	550	1,020	1,570	415

As may be seen from this table, the turnover in supplies rose 3·3 times in the course of four years, and the sale about 7·8 times. In 1926/27 the total turnover of primary co-operatives stood at 1,570 million roubles. The network of primary agricultural societies is occupied predominantly with the sale of agricultural produce, which increases from year to year.

[1] One pound sterling is equal to 9·50 roubles.

The agricultural co-operatives took up the organisation of agricultural credit later than any other task. This is explained by the fact that there were special difficulties in the solution of this problem, principally, however, that a stable currency had first to be created as a basis. With the allocation of certain small state grants to agriculture, the co-operatives set to work on credit operations and soon achieved a great development of their activities in this direction.

The balance of loan accounts gives the following figures: On October 1, 1925—79.28 million roubles; on October 1, 1926—129.03 million roubles; on October 1, 1927—259.11 million roubles; on July 1, 1928—370.2 million roubles. As may be seen from these figures, the rise in the total of loans shows unbroken progress, and this total has increased more than three and a half times in the course of three years, and has reached the considerable figure of 370.2 million roubles. The loan operations do not only show an absolute increase, but also an increase relatively for each co-operative society —that is, for each co-operative member.

This increase in loans is of the greatest importance for the reconstruction and further development of peasant economy. The loans made by agricultural co-operatives all serve explicitly productive purposes, and are never applied to unproductive ends or for the personal use of the peasant. Of the loans made in 1924/25, 95 per cent. were used for production and 4·1 per cent. for consumption. In 1927/28 99·1 per cent. were employed for production and less than 1 per cent. for consumption.

But the provision of credit is not the sole or main function of agricultural co-operation, which consists rather in its trading activities. The supply and sale turnover of the local agricultural unions are shown by the following table:

	In Million Roubles.		Total.	
	Supply.	Sale.	Million Roubles.	Percentage.
1923/24 ..	123	127	250	100
1924/25 ..	193	200	393	157
1925/26 ..	245	437	682	273
1926/27 ..	315	790	1,105	442

The trading turnover of the Central Unions is shown by the following table:

	In Million Roubles.		Total.	
	Supply.	Sale.	Million Roubles.	Percentage.
1923/24 ..	25	55	80	100
1924/25 ..	28	149	177	221
1925/26 ..	61	258	319	399
1926/27 ..	89	366	455	569

By comparing the turnover of the Central Unions with that of the primary societies and the local unions, it will be seen that the first mentioned has developed with much greater intensity than the turnover of either of the latter. In the course of four years the turnover of the unions increased 7½ times, that of the primary societies 7 times, and that of the central unions more than 5½ times. The total turnover of the whole agricultural co-operative system in the U.S.S.R. stands, in millions of roubles, as follows:

			Supply.	Sale.	Total.
1923/24 ..	..	..	314	394	768
1924/25 ..	..	..	553	718	1,271
1925/26 ..	..	..	748	1,386	2,134
1926/27 ..	..	..	954	2,176	3,130

The turnover of the agricultural co-operatives for 1927/28 has not yet been published. The data for nine months, however, allows us to assume that the general turnover of all agricultural societies and unions together for 1927/28 will not be less than 4,250,000 roubles.[1]

IV. THE CENTRAL UNIONS

In order to make clear the position and activities of agricultural co-operation in the individual branches of agriculture, it will be well here to go more fully into the work and character of the various central unions of the agricultural co-operatives.

THE " SELSKOSOJUS "

is the all-Russian union of agricultural co-operative societies for supplying the peasants with the means of production: agricultural machinery, seeds, etc. This union, founded in 1921 as the apical union for all agricultural co-operatives, functioned in the first years of its existence, as has already been explained, as the general purposes central organisation of the agricultural co-operative movement, and served the local unions in an organisational as well as a trading capacity. The specialisation of agricultural co-operation led to the separation of the marketing functions— the handling, for example, of flax, butter, tobacco, eggs, etc.—from the sphere of Selskosojus activities and their transference to the newly formed central unions for special branches, such as Lnocentr, Maslocentr, Centrotabaksojus and others. Later, when in 1926 the

[1] The total turnover is reached by adding together the turnover of each of the three above-mentioned groups. It consequently includes a double turnover in the last figure.

19

organisational leadership of the entire agricultural co-operative movement was transferred to the council which had just been elected by the individual central unions (reorganised in 1927 as the "Union of Agricultural Co-operative Unions," uniting all the central as well as the large local unions), the only function remaining to the Selskosojus was that of a supplying centre for the agricultural co-operatives. The output of agricultural produce was taken over from Selskosojus by the newly formed Central Unions. Even in 1925 the turnover in produce was as high as 73 per cent. of the total. By 1926, however, produce was only 38 per cent. as against 62 per cent. of supplies. From 1927 onwards no produce was handled by the Selskosojus. As early as 1923 the turnover in supplies began to grow considerably. Taking the figure in 1923 as 100, in 1924 it had risen to 120, in 1925 to 177, in 1926 to 330, and in 1927 to 480. Thus, the total turnover of Selskosojus as supplier of agricultural requirements had multiplied nearly five times in four years.

The dealings of the Selskosojus with the co-operative movement extend over the whole Soviet Union with the exception of the Ukraine, but are specially concerned with the following regions: (1) The central industrial area (governments of Moscow, Tver, Jaroslav, Kostroma, Vladimir); (2) the North Caucasus; (3) the Central Black Earth Region (governments of Voronesh, Tambov, Kursk, etc.); (4) the Ural Region; (5) the Lower Volga Region; and (6) Siberia.

The list of goods which the Selskosojus supplies to its affiliated co-operatives is multifarious. It includes agricultural machinery and tools, tractors, spare parts, various agricultural appliances, ironware (tin-roofing and galvanised sheet-iron, nails, pots and pans, etc.), building materials, chemical manure, fungicides and insecticides, electro-technical materials, etc.

IN THE SOVIET UNION

As central purchasing union of R.S.F.S.R., the Selskosojus unites the greater part of the agricultural co-operative societies and unions. On April 1, 1928, it numbered amongst its members 21 regional and 139 local unions. Since 1926 the supplying of local co-operatives has been carried on on a strictly co-operative basis, firm orders being received from the unions. The general results of supply operations 1922-26 are shown by the following figures:

Type of Goods.	Sales (1922-26) in Million Roubles.	Percentage of Total.
Agricultural machinery and tools ..	27.30	36·7
Tractors	8.72	11·1
Metal goods	26.53	35·2
Chemicals and drugs	2.41	3·2
Means of destroying pests	1.30	1·7
Seeds..	9.44	11·4
Total	75.70	100·0

As shown in this table, the major portion of the turn-over, actually 36·4 per cent., consists of agricultural machinery and tools, followed by metal goods, with 35·2 per cent. Operations in different types of goods do not show any uniform rate of progression. The supply of tractors has developed most rapidly. First reaching a considerable figure in 1924, it has increased 4½ times in the course of four years (1.20 million roubles in 1924 as against 5.19 million roubles in 1926). A very significant increase, almost fourfold, has taken place over this period in the turnover of agricultural machinery and tools, as well as in chemicals. The supply of seeds (transferred in 1928 to a special central union, the " Semenovodsojus ") has increased 3½ times during the same period, while the supply of materials to combat pests has doubled.

AGRICULTURAL CO-OPERATION

In connection with the provision of the land with agricultural machines and implements, special attention should be paid to combined agricultural machines and tractors. These serve to bring agriculture to a higher level and establish it on a technical and industrial basis. In the period before the war, about half the demand for agricultural machinery and implements was met by imports from abroad. Thus, in 1912, of the total purchases of 116.17 million roubles, 63.55 million roubles were expended on agricultural machinery and tools from abroad, which equals 54·7 per cent. of the total. In 1913 the purchases were 109.19 million roubles and the imports 48·68 million roubles, or 44·6 per cent. After the revolution, the import of agricultural machinery still played an important part. The pressing need to industrialise agriculture at a period when the total demand for tools and machinery could not be met with the products of home industry, made imports from abroad a necessity. These are shown in the following figures:

	Total.	*Imported.*
	(In Thousands of Gold Roubles.)	
1923	14.664	2·817
1924	22.545	4·741
1925	61.266	21.370
1926	107.714	37.271

The growth of home production of agricultural machinery hindered the development of the corresponding import in 1927 and 1928. Home production of agricultural machinery in 1927/28 amounted to 201 per cent. of the pre-war production. The demand for agricultural machinery by the peasant farmers is growing rapidly—*i.e.*, in 1926/27 there was agricultural machinery to the value of 9.90 roubles for each 100 hectares, and by the end of 1928 this figure rose to 12 roubles. Therefore, in spite of the extraordinarily rapid development of home industry, the importance of the imports has not diminished.

The percentage relationship between imported goods and the products of home industry, as far as concerns the supplies of the Selskosojus, are made clear in the next table:

	1925.		1926.	
	Imports.	*Home Production.*	*Imports.*	*Home Production.*
	Per Cent.	*Per Cent.*	*Per Cent.*	*Per Cent.*
Agricultural machinery and tools	34	66	28·7	71·3
Tractors	100	—	98·2	1·8
Chemical manures ..	89	11	86	14
Means of combating pests	76	24	93	7
Various seeds	42	58	38	62
Building materials, etc...	7	93	9·8	90·2
Total	36	64	26·5	73·5

As may be seen from this table, the Selskosojus carried out more than a quarter of its purchase for 1926 abroad.

As will be shown, the Selskosojus, as central co-operative supply department fills an important place in the general import of agricultural requirements. Its share in the total imports of the Soviet Union has steadily increased: in 1925 it stood at 11·3 per cent., in 1926 at 18·6 per cent., in 1927 at 36 per cent., in 1928 at 46 per cent. In comparison with the rate of increase of the total import of the U.S.S.R., the imports of the Selskosojus have advanced much more rapidly.

AGRICULTURAL CO-OPERATION

It is natural that the imports of Selskosojus, the central supply department, should develop more rapidly than those of the other special unions of the agricultural co-operative movement, as Selskosojus has gradually concentrated all imports in its hands. Thus, in 1924, its imports were 65·8 per cent. of the total imports of the Central Unions; in 1925 the share of the Selskosojus had risen to 66·9 per cent., and in 1926 to 84 per cent. In 1927 and 1928 only Maslocentr (the central union of the dairying industry) took any considerable part in the imports, and those principally dairy requisites, separators and barrelstaves.

The Selskosojus carries on the purchase of imported goods through the foreign representatives of the agricultural co-operatives, being through them in direct business relation with foreign producers and suppliers.

For home products the Selskosojus meets its requirements principally from the state industries, with whom it concludes large general agreements for different kinds of agricultural requirements.

The principal customers of the Selskosojus are the co-operative unions and their members. Only a very small proportion of the sales of certain goods are disposed of otherwise.

The exact figures for these ever-growing supplies, divided according to individual classes of goods, are as follows: The turnover for agricultural machinery and tools stood in 1921-22 at 728,000 roubles; 1923, 1,399,000 roubles; 1924, 3,374,000 roubles; 1925, 7,858,000 roubles; 1926, 13,915,000 roubles; and 1927, 35,000,000 roubles. A turnover of 66,000,000 roubles is anticipated for the year 1928. The turnover in tractors stood in 1925 at 2,248,600 roubles; in 1926 at 5,193,500 roubles, and in 1927 at 5,340,000 roubles. The supply of the population with seeds was carried on by the

Selskosojus until the end of 1927. In 1928 it handed over this business to the newly formed central union of seed-growers, Semenovodsojus. The supply of manures carried on by the Selskosojus reached the following amounts: 1921, 6,200 cwt.; 1923, 12,300 cwt.; 1924, 32,800 cwt.; 1925, 54,100 cwt.; 1926, 89,400 cwt.; and 1927, 127,900 cwt. The turnover in heavy metals has been, in 1922, 707,000 roubles; in 1924, 3,922,000 roubles; in 1925, 6,124,000 roubles; in 1926/27, 14,816,000 roubles; in 1927/8, 25,135,000 roubles.

In 1928 Selskosojus together with Khlebocentr formed several tractor colonies which ploughed the peasants' land for a fixed charge. These tractor colonies ploughed great areas of land, levelling the surface, facilitating cultivation and increasing the yield (the average peasant harvest was increased by 30 to 40 per cent.). There were in 1928, 14 colonies with 327 tractors, which ploughed about 60,000 hectares of peasant land. Mention must also be made of the establishment of hiring stations where the peasants can hire a machine without having to apply to private persons whose terms are exorbitant.

As explained above, the central co-operative unions have almost entirely taken over the sale of the agricultural produce of their members. The Selskosojus, on the other hand, has not yet found it possible to concentrate the entire supply of its affiliated unions and members into its own hands. This is partly owing to the fact that until 1926 the Selskosojus, besides its own work, was also occupied with the sale of agricultural produce. The lack of the necessary credit, in part also from abroad, further militated against the Selskosojus devoting itself sufficiently in the years 1923-26 to the general supply of co-operative agriculture with the means of production.

AGRICULTURAL CO-OPERATION

The supply of machinery and tools to the agricultural co-operatives in 1926 was as high as 65·8 per cent. of the total supply to the peasants; the supply of tractors, 42 per cent. In 1927 the supply of machines rose to 70 per cent., and that of tractors to 53 per cent. In the Ukraine the supply of machines is entirely in the hand of the co-operatives. In metal goods, the supply to the whole agricultural co-operative movement was a little over one-third of the total supplies on the agricultural market. The first to be supplied with machinery are the productive societies: tractor societies and societies for common use of agricultural machinery and in particular communes and artels. Selskosojus ascertained from experience that the machinery and appliances can be fully utilised only through the united productive societies.

The following is a table of the growth in the trading turnover of the Selskosojus in the last four years (in gold roubles):

1923/24	..	..	..	39,883.7	100
1924/25	..	..	..	48,076.4	120·5
1925/26	..	..	..	67,384.3	In percentages of 1923-24	168·9
1926/27	..	..	..	68,710.6	172·2
1927/28	..	..	..	90,100.0	226·7

It is observable that the trading turnover of the Selskosojus has grown from year to year in spite of the fact that precisely during the period under discussion a number of operations have been transferred to the newly formed central unions.

MASLOCENTR: THE ALL-RUSSIAN UNION OF DAIRYING CO-OPERATIVES.

Maslocentr, as the head organisation ar.d central union of the agricultural dairying (milk and creamery) co-operatives, acts as a productive and marketing organisation which devotes itself principally to the organisation of dairying, butter and cheese making and the disposal of its products.

Maslocentr was formed in June, 1924, and established itself on a three-grade system: (1) the primary co-operatives (milk and butter-making artels); (2) the local, district unions; (3) the central union. For Siberia and the Urals there exists, in consideration for their special local conditions, a deviation from this system, in that another grade is admitted, and regional unions are allowed for Siberia and the Ural. All co-operatives in the dairy industry work almost entirely in their own special department, market fresh milk for the members, control the whole process of production and sale of butter and cheese and improve by various methods the dairy cattle, milk husbandry and processing of milk of their members and their associations.

The milk comes from the peasant's farm to be processed at an artel depot, whence it is turned out in the form of butter, cheese, etc., or in a fresh condition. The dairying artels have not merely the processing and sale of milk in their hands, but they also work for an improvement in dairy herds, for rational care and feeding of milch cows, for the production of special feeding stuffs and a technical improvement in butter making. In this way the artels act as the organising centres for the dairying industry in their neighbourhood.

Their activities also extend to an improvement in the methods of processing milk and the supplying of their members with pedigree stock and concentrated foods through the district union, and further, with the organisation of exhibitions of milch cows, etc.

The district dairying union bestows its special attention on the disposal of milk products, on agricultural instruction amongst dairymen, and further takes steps to improve and raise the co-operative dairy farms. With the last object in view, it arranges courses for the training of professional butter-makers. The district union has control over a number of agronomist-zoötechnicians, organises exhibitions of dairy cattle and supplies the artels with modern means of production.

Maslocentr, which as headquarters represents the interests of the whole organisation, devotes itself principally to the rationalisation of the whole peasant dairying industry and the technical improvement of the creamery business. With this object, Maslocentr calls special conferences in the large towns and in various villages, promotes the organisation of special cow-testing societies and undertakes a number of measures to secure the rationalisation of production. The dairying co-operatives are supplied by Maslocentr with special machinery, dairying sundries, tools and materials, for which purpose it established its own plant, producing different kinds of dairy utensils. In so far as the needs of the members are not covered by its own production, Maslocentr imports creamery plant, dairying sundries, laboratory requirements and other articles from abroad to aid the progress of the dairying industry.

The development of Maslocentr's system of affiliated local unions and co-operatives is shown by the following table:

	Oct. 1, 1925.	Oct. 1, 1926.	Oct. 1, 1927.	April 1, 1928.
Number of unions	61	60	60	52
Number of co-operatives	5,072	5,874	6,372	6,175
Number of members (thousands)	798·7	950·8	1,310·3	1,431·4
Number of cows (thousands) ..	1,642·0	1,992·2	2,085	2,145
Average number of members in a co-operative	157	162	201	214

Of the 6,175 co-operatives, affiliated to Maslocentr, 4,930 are special and 1,245 general purposes organisations, which are engaged in the dairying industry only as a side-line. Further, there are affiliated to Maslocentr, 7,696 co-operative dairy plants, of which about 6,000 are creameries, 711 cheese factories and nearly 1,000 carry on other businesses.

The activities of the dairying co-operative movement organised in the Masolcentr are carried on principally in five productive regions: (1) The region of " Export-butter " (Siberia and Ural), with 62 per cent. of the co-operatives; (2) the region of sweet cream butter (Viatka-Vetluga and the northern region); (3) the region of cheese production (Government of Kostroma, Smolensk, North Caucasus); (4) the region of mixed production (butter, cheese and sometimes also milk); and (5) the region of fresh milk production (in the neighbourhood of consuming centres). A remarkable fact in connection with the activities of the dairying co-operatives is that 92 per cent. of the total butter production takes place in co-operative creameries. The bulk of the butter produced passes from the artels to the local unions on a co-operative basis; only a trivial amount goes to various purchasers.

The development of production since the formation of Maslocentr can be traced as follows through butter production, which forms the principal manufactured product of Maslocentr:

Butter Production.	Double Cwt.	Percentage of 1924/25.
1924-25	258,430	100·0
1925-26	349,093	135·1
1926-27	485,295	187 8
1927-28	486,100	188·0

AGRICULTURAL CO-OPERATION

The position held by Maslocentr amongst the other butter-collecting organisations will be shown by the following figures: In 1924-25, Maslocentr marketed 53·8 per cent. of the butter on the market; in 1925-26, 60·8 per cent.; 1926-27, 67·5 per cent.; and in 1927-28, 68·2 per cent.

Of the above stated total of butter produced, the following amounts were exported by Maslocentr abroad:

Butter Export.	Exported by Maslocentr in Double Cwt. ($\frac{1}{10}$ Ton).	Percentage of 1924/25.	Percentage of Total Butter Export from U.S.S.R.
1924/25 ..	108,705	100·0	44·7
1925/26 ..	119,825	110·2	56·1
1926/27 ..	180,197	165·8	65·0
1927/28 ..	186,011	170·3	69·3

Cheese production shows a similar growth in the trading activities of Maslocentr:

	1924/25.	1925/26.	1926/27.
Sale of cheese through Maslocentr (double cwt.)	33,600	42,098	56,115
Percentage of 1924/25	100·0	125·3	167·0

In addition to butter and cheese, casein is also manufactured by Maslocentr. In 1926/27 production stood at 3,343 double hundredweights, which was consumed in the country. The principal users are the state industrial undertakings, especially wood-working and aeroplane construction.

The fact that the dairying co-operatives now handle by far the greater portion of the peasant's output is due to co-operative methods of sale and the payment of

30

bonus on sales. When the peasant hands over his produce, he receives the average local price. If the goods are sold in the central market or abroad at a higher price, the peasant receives the price difference after the sale has been effected. This is called " co-operative additional payment " and is equivalent to bonus or dividend on sales. In this way the additional payments of the Maslocentr amounted in 1924-25 to the sum of 1,355,000 roubles; in 1925-26 to 1,263,000 roubles; and in 1926-27 to 1,500,000 roubles.

The development in the dairying co-operatives has not shown itself only in the extension of selling operations. There has been progress also in the organisational and technical spheres, in the co-operative transformation of peasant economy and in the improvement in the processes of production.

As is known, the earlier co-operative creameries were usually on a low level, from the technical point of view. The bad construction of the creameries and the poor quality of the raw material resulted in a low quality product. Consequently, it was obviously one of the chief tasks of the present dairy co-operatives to rationalise the co-operative dairying industry and butter-production. The effort next found expression in the mechanisation of the industry, in the supersession of the old small creameries and the erection of new mechanised creamery plants. This activity has developed with especial vigour since 1926. In 1924-25, 468 creameries were erected and 296 renovated; in 1925-26, 683 new ones were built and 413 renovated; in 1926-27, 768 were built and 314 renovated; in 1927-28, 830 new creameries were built. In the course of four years (1924-25—1927-28) 25.3 million roubles has been expended in the construction and renovation of co-operative creameries, cheese factories, etc.

A work of no less importance has been performed by

the dairy co-operatives system for the increase and improvement of the output through the utilisation of by-products so that a higher standard of production may be attained by rational and intensive management.

This is newly developed work with no precedent, for the dairy co-operatives, in the pre-revolutionary period, performed hardly any agricultural-technical work. In 1925-26, 1,700,000 poods[1] of concentrated feeding stuffs were distributed amongst the members of the dairying co-operatives; in 1926-27, 3·5 million poods, and in 1927-28 over 8 million poods.

A few figures may be added which will give the progress of the turnover of Maslocentr for the period of its existence:

1924-25	..	..	..	38.2 million roubles.
1925-26	..	..	..	53.9 ,, ,,
1926-27	..	..	..	67.7 ,, ,,
1927-28	..	..	..	111.0 ,, ,,

In the total turnover of all central unions Maslocentr took the third place in 1927-28, following Selskosojus and Khlebocentr (the grain union).

Zhivotnovodsojus: All-Russian Central Union of Agricultural Livestock Co-operatives.

Zhivotnovodsojus is the central union of agricultural co-operative societies for the manufacture and sale of the produce of cattle and other animals, and was founded in May, 1927. The principal object of the Central Union is to promote stock-keeping through its affiliated local unions and co-operatives, and through this to rebuild peasant economy and increase its turnover. This last object is attained by the Zhivotnovodsojus through increased output, through the scientific pro-

---

[1] One pood = 36 lbs.

cessing of animal produce and through the supply to the peasants of improved breeding stock. Before the formation of Zhivotnovodsojus, Selskosojus undertook the disposal of animal products and the other activities mentioned above.

The sphere of operations of the Zhivotnovodsojus includes the following products: (1) furs, hides, Persian lambskins; (2) cattle and meat; (3) leather; (4) all kinds of wool; (5) raw sinews and casings, bristles and horsehair; (6) bacon; (7) semi-raw materials, with which are classed treated sinews and bristles. The Zhivotnovodsojus does not concern itself with dairy produce, eggs or poultry, which come under the control of the Maslocentr or the Ptizevodsojus.

On the productive side, the Zhivotnovodsojus is occupied with the supply to the co-operatively organised peasants of breeding stock and the organisation of stock-breeding, through the establishment of points of assembly, breeding stations, stud-farms, herdbooks, etc., also with the erection of concerns for the processing of animal raw materials, bacon factories, slaughterhouses, cold-storage factories and workshops for the treating of sinews, wool-cleansing centres, etc.

Animal raw materials passing through the agricultural co-operative system to the Zhivotnovodsojus for disposal, are sold by the latter to the state industrial syndicate, to joint stock companies and to the central union of the " home industries " co-operatives; a portion remains for export abroad. The export of animal raw materials is for the most part carried on independently by the Zhivotnovodsojus. Sales abroad take place through the foreign representatives of the agricultural co-operatives, especially in the chief articles, such as furs and Persian lambs' skins, bacon, etc. An appreciable portion of the exported products, particularly raw leather, bristles, sinews and by-products, such as horns, hoofs, horsehair, etc., finds a market through the Gostorg (State-Export-Company), through mixed companies and through the trade representatives of the U.S.S.R.

The turnover in animal raw materials, already increasing under Selskosojus, now shows a steady growth under Zhivotnovodsojus. At the same time, an admitted weakening is shown in the turnover of certain articles whose origin may be traced to a corresponding weakening in the production of the raw material in question:

	In Thousand Roubles.			
	1924-25.	1925-26.	1926-27.	1927-28.
1. Meat	4,824·7	6,816.5	11,988.4	41,298.0
2. Bacon	—	—	234.4	1,989.0
3. Furs	11,180.0	8,285.0	9,425.0	14,108.0
4. Wool	2,913.7	5,048.1	9,037.7	21,685.0
5. Horses	1,116.9	3,812.0	3,315.3	1,687.0

The total turnover for 1927/28 amounted to 98,807,000 roubles.

The importance of the agricultural co-operatives in supplying industry with raw materials increases from year to year and stands in percentage relation to the total supplies of all supplying organisations as follows:

	1924-25.	1925-26.	1926-27.	1927-28.
Wool	12·3	31·0	48·8	55·3
Leather ..	3·0	7·0	12·0	18·0

The mutual relations between Zhivotnovodsojus and the industries receiving its products rest on the conclusion of general agreements. Thus, for the year 1927-28, a whole series of agreements have been entered into between Zhivotnovodsojus on the one hand and the Industrial Syndicates, the mixed companies, the Central Union of Industrial Co-operatives and the consumers' co-operatives on the other.

The export of animal raw materials was begun by the agricultural co-operative societies in 1924, that is in the year following their first independent appearance on the foreign market. The export of animal raw materials by the Zhivotnovodsojus (furs, bacon, sinews, bristles, etc.) reached the sum of £600,000 in 1926-27, and £1,300,000 in 1927-28. The Zhivotnovodsojus takes its place as follows amongst the other organisations in the Soviet Union engaged in the production of the articles named below:

	Percentages of the General Production of all other Organisations.	
	1925-26.	1926-27.
Meat products	15·0	26
Raw leather	17·5	29
Wool	44·0	55
Persian lambs' skins	35·0	60
Furs	15·0	22
Sinews	4·7	5·7

The proportion of local unions engaged in the production of animal raw materials increases from year to year in the following proportions:

	1923.	1924.	1925.	1926.	1927.	1928.
Number of unions producing animal raw materials (exclusive of dairy and poultry produce)	40	64	85	110	108	96

AGRICULTURAL CO-OPERATION

Of the 96 unions which are at present affiliated to the Zhivotnovodsojus, 35 are republican and regional unions and 61 district unions. A majority of these are general purposes unions; the special unions number 32. The growth of special stock-keeping co-operatives (primary) in 1926-27 may be seen from the following tables:

	July 1, 1926.	July 1, 1927.	April 1, 1928.
Sheep-farming co-operatives	240	400	550
Horse-breeding ,, ...	420	750	874
Pig-keeping ,, ...	14	127	140
Cattle-breeding ,, ...	—	200	190
General purposes, stock-keeping co-operatives and various	300	520	2,104
Total	974	1,597	3,838

It must be noted that the majority of these co-operatives are nothing but small primary societies whose main aim is to improve the breed of their cattle: 3,838 societies embrace 147,000 peasant households. Their trade turnover is not large yet, but it is growing rapidly. On the other hand, the development of special unions may be shown as follows:

On May 1, 1927, there were only 9 special unions.

On October 1, 1928, there were 32 special unions, of which

2 were sheep-farming unions,

4 horse-breeding unions, and

26 mixed stock-keeping unions.

For zoötechnical objects, a special agro-zoötechnical fund was formed for all stock-breeding co-operatives. Certain fixed percentage deductions from the sales turnover are made for the benefit of this fund, but in the first year of the existence of Zhivotnovodsojus, no sum worth mentioning has yet been accumulated.

Within the compass of its own existing means, and with the credit obtained for this purpose, Zhivotnovodsojus has purchased 948 pedigree rams and 1,313 sheep, chiefly of the merino breed, and distributed them in the sheep-breeding areas (Crimea, the autonomous Republic of the Volga Germans, the autonomous Republic of the Buriats, Siberia, etc.); further, it has established 16 pedigree flocks in the R.S.F.S.R., consisting of 500 sheep and 20 rams.

For the purpose of supplying concentrated feeding-stuffs to the peasants, there has been established between the Zhivotnovodsojus and the state oil and fat syndicate, a depot for the supply of oil-cake to the individual unions.

One of the principal activities of the organisation is the processing of animal products. The construction of factories for this purpose is slow and requires large financial resources. In addition to this the Zhivotnovodsojus has also to improve those concerns which it took over from the Selskosojus as well as to begin the construction of fresh concerns. The Zhivotnovodsojus received from Selskosojus two bacon factories in Voronesh and Pokrovsk, built in 1925, as well as a number of sinew workshops. Two bacon factories—in Viatka and Krasnodar—are in course of construction and will start work in 1929.

Normal work in the first-named undertakings began in the 1927-28 season, and an improvement in the quality of the product and a rationalisation of the industry was thereby attained. In bacon production, the Zhivotnovodsojus does not confine its action to the organisation of a scientific slaughtering of pigs and a correct processing of the carcasses, but also sees that on the farms of co-operatively organised peasants only well-adapted

37

pigs should be selected for slaughter and only suitable feeding stuffs should be fed to them. An accelerated construction of bacon factories is anticipated for the forthcoming years, and further factories and workshops will be erected for the processing of sinews, for which purpose the present equipment is very inadequate.

PTIZEVODSOJUS: CENTRAL UNION OF THE POULTRY CO-OPERATIVES.

In the period before the war, the production of eggs and poultry formed an important branch of Russian agriculture, and the export of these products was considerable. During the world war and the civil war, poultry keeping in the Soviet Union suffered great losses. Almost all poultry farms in the theatre of war or its immediate neighbourhood were destroyed, and, further, many birds were so weakened by the lack of feeding stuffs that poultry breeding fell into complete decay. The recovery of the land which followed, the resurrection of agriculture and the development of its output also exercised a favourable influence on agricultural poultry-farming, so that this type of production gradually regained its former importance, both in the national trade and in the economy of the peasant.

The principal task which the Ptizevodsojus then set before it was the organisation of output and the processing of poultry products on a co-operative basis, as well as the support of the peasants going in for poultry breeding and its allied occupations.

Ptizevodsojus carries on its work for the most part through the agricultural general purposes co-operatives, whilst relying on the direct support of the co-operative unions and the agricultural credit co-operatives. It also relies on the so-called " Kooptiza " (the co-operative poultry keepers' societies), which form a kind of contracting co-operative so that its members, though not peasants, are included amongst those of the Ptizevodsojus and the local agricultural co-operative unions. In 1928 four special poultry unions were for the first time organised in the North Caucasus (Rostov), the Central Black Earth Region (Voronesh), Tartar Republic (Kasan) and Bashkiz Republic (Ufa).

The poultry breeding system is being developed by the organisation of small poultry artels (comprised mostly of women and very often of women only). These artels are affiliated to the so-called "Station groups" for the purpose of the disposal of the eggs and poultry.

The structure of the Ptizevodsojus is shown in the following table:

	Oct. 1, 1926.	Oct. 1, 1927.	April 1, 1928.
Number of unions	27	28	29
Number of primary co-operatives affiliated to them[1]	513	642	1,800

It must be observed that the agricultural co-operative movement before the war paid practically no attention to poultry and that the agricultural co-operatives of Soviet Russia were pioneers in the co-operative organisation of peasants engaged in poultry keeping. It testifies to the difficulty of the task that peasant villages are widely scattered over the vast territories of the Soviet Union and that in contrast with foreign countries, such as Denmark, only a small number of fowls are to be found in each farmyard.

[1] Poultry artels are not included in the first two columns, as then they did not play an important part. However, they are included in the data for April 1, 1928, making in all 214, with 25,000 peasant families affiliated. On October 1, 1928, their number rose to 520 artels.

AGRICULTURAL CO-OPERATION

The agricultural co-operatives have undertaken the collection of poultry produce since 1922, at first using the general purposes societies for that purpose. In the following year, simultaneously with the general recovery in agricultural output, especially of poultry produce, special poultry co-operatives were formed for the first time.

The Ptizevodsojus works principally with the unions and only exceptionally draws direct from the primary co-operatives for the disposal of poultry produce. The collection of eggs and poultry by the Ptizevodsojus system is carried on by means of agreements between Ptizevodsojus, on the one hand, and the unions, or the large co-operative poultry farms, on the other. The unions transfer a portion of the supply to the local co-operative by analogous agreements; the remainder is secured by the unions' own system. The development of the egg and poultry co-operatives (R.S.F.S.R.) for the period from 1923-27 took place as follows:

	Egg Production.		Egg Export.	
	Truck Load.	Percentage of Total Production.	Truck Load.	Percentage of Export of other Organisations.
1924-25 ..	919	15·5	154	—
1925-26 ..	723	29·0	240	19·7
1926-27 ..	2,848	43·4	1,154	37·7
1927-28 ..	4,400	45·0	1,870	41·7

Poultry (Various) by Truck Load.					Production.
1922-23 ..	..	..	..	..	8
1923-24 ..	..	..	..	..	12
1924-25 ..	..	..	..	..	72
1925-26 ..	..	..	..	..	100
1926-27 ..	..	..	..	..	295
1927-28 ..	..	..	..	..	752

The upward movement of the output and the receipts shows a rapid development, especially in the last period of the activity of the agricultural co-operatives.

The collection of poultry products is sometimes carried on by the agricultural co-operatives, through special collecting agents throughout the area of the co-operative in question or else through special small egg and poultry artels, who collect the produce in their own colonies and are affiliated, technically either as egg-collecting stations or feeding-stuff depots.

The general purposes agricultural co-operatives, as well as those specially concerned with poultry, assemble the eggs and poultry submitted to them and either forward it direct to the local union or carry out a preliminary grading and systematic packing. The Union puts the goods supplied to it into a saleable condition.

In describing the general work of the Ptizevodsojus, its technical agricultural work must not be left unnoticed as in this respect it plays an important part amongst the agricultural co-operatives. Ptizevodsojus has established breeding centres for the purpose of increasing the output and improving the quality of eggs and poultry, through which birds of a good strain are introduced from abroad and distributed amongst the special unions and co-operatives; the latter are also supplied with incubators and similar appliances for poultry breeding. The home production of incubators is being gradually introduced. In the last two years the establishment of feeding and packing depots, cold storage warehouses, incubators and model farms has proceeded rapidly.

In 1928, 53 large feeding and packing stations were built with a capacity each of fattening 30,000 chickens simultaneously. The season allows of 3 batches of chickens, making a total 90,000 fattened during the season.

In many parts of the country attempts at metisation and a complete elimination of unproductive breeders have been made, further measures have been taken to accelerate the transport of eggs from their place of origin to the collecting station. The utilisation of egg by-products, and especially the methods of scientific mass feeding in the agricultural poultry-feeding establishments, are thoroughly investigated in the laboratory. All these measures will serve to place poultry-keeping on a new modern technical basis and to expedite its development.

A subsidiary branch of poultry-keeping—feathers and down—has not up till now played any prominent part in the Ptizevodsojus system. The feather and down factory in Zaraisk, with an annual capacity of 5,000 tons, is principally supplied by the agricultural co-operatives with raw materials from dead poultry. The co-operatives are compelled to hand over feathers and down to the Ptizevodsojus. The export of these products first began in 1926. The export in the coming year will be increased by the construction of new factories.

LNOCENTR: CENTRAL UNION OF FLAX AND HEMP GROWERS CO-OPERATIVES.

Lnocentr was founded in September, 1921, as the central union of flax and hemp growers in the Non-Black Earth Region of the R.S.F.S.R., the area of flax thread cultivation. The principal districts for flax-growing are concentrated (1) in the western provinces (Smolensk, Tver, Pskov and White Russia), which supply flax mainly for export; and (2) in the north-eastern provinces (Kostroma, Jaroslav, Viatka, etc.) supplying flax to the home industry. During recent years flax growing has developed in new districts though the principal supplies are still drawn from the above named. In addition, Lnocentr was joined by the hemp growers of the governments of Orel, Kursk, Briansk, Pensa and other places in which hemp production is concentrated. The Lnocentr relies in its work on the local general purposes co-operatives of the hemp and flax areas which are concerned with the production of hemp and flax fibre and seeds. Three flax and two hemp unions were organised for the first time in 1928.

The united flax co-operatives represent an harmoniously constructed system whose individual members are linked together, each carrying out their stipulated work and all together working for the development of mass production. Amongst the individual members, there is a sharp division of labour correspondent to the division between flax and hemp.

Production is based on three principal functions: the collection of the fibre is undertaken by the primary co-operatives; the Union, formed by a dozen or so co-operatives, undertakes the pooling of the individual contributions which are graded in the mass and put into a saleable condition for the requirements of the home as well as the foreign market. At the same time, this system does not exclude the direct acquisition of flax by the union. The Lnocentr, which is at the head of all the flax co-operatives, disposes of the entire output.

Lnocentr makes contracts for sowing flax, making the peasant advances in money or kind (principally seeds and manure). These contracts guarantee to the peasants the disposal of their flax at a certain price and to Lnocentr a certain quantity of flax. They help the peasants as well as the co-operatives and the flax industry to prepare plans for their future work. The output is disposed of both at home to the government industries, and abroad.

The development of the operations of Lnocentr is shown by the following table:

			Flax.		
			Tons.	*Percentage of 1922-23.*	*Percentage of Total Flax on the Market.*
1922-23	..	..	8,922·0	100	12·1
1923-24	..	..	11,477·0	128	17·1
1924-25	..	..	24,739·3	276	20·2
1925-26	..	..	42,031·8	470·5	24·4
1926-27	..	..	43,514·6	485·2	34·6
1927-28	..	..	66,702·7	706	54·8

The following table shows the relations between home and foreign sales:

					Sales of Flax to Industry.	
					Home.	*Foreign.*
1922-23	..	..	..	..	4,098 tons	4,754 tons
1923-24	..	..	..	..	4,858 ,,	6,455 ,,
1924-25	..	..	..	..	11,555 ,,	13,173 ,,
1925-26	..	..	..	..	21,623 ,,	20,820 ,,
1926-27	..	..	..	..	27,372 ,,	15,672 ,,
1927-28	..	..	..	..	48,335 ,,	15,765 ,,

These figures show a decrease in the export of flax during the last two years as compared with 1925-26 which is chiefly due to the fact that Lnocentr has been supplying its own country with great quantities of flax to meet the growing demands of its flax industry.

The collection and distribution of flax seeds has developed even more rapidly. There is also an increase in the operations in hemp, but not in such a high degree as in flax and flax seeds.

				Output of Flax Seed.	Output of Hemp.
1922-23	..	..	..	3,491·8 tons	3,399·8 tons
1923-24	..	..	..	7,327·8 ,,	1,638·0 ,,
1924-25	..	..	..	28,360·6 ,,	3,042·6 ,,
1925-26	..	..	..	41,032·8 ,,	6,065·5 ,,
1926-27	..	..	..	57,377·0 ,,	12,427 8 ,,
1927-28	..	..	..	Figures not available	34,926·1 ,,

In the year 1924-25 the collection of hempseed was also begun, and in 1924-25 about 1,700 tons, in 1925-26, 3,197 tons and in 1926-27, 4,541 tons were collected.

In addition to the activities outlined above, the Lnocentr also undertakes technical agricultural work, by which it seeks to build up and ameliorate the flax-growing industry so as to secure a qualitative improvement in the product and an increase in the crop-yield. For this purpose Lnocentr collects every year from the local co-operatives the best and most productive seed from the planting area of Flachs-Dolgunetz, cleans it at its seed-cleaning stations, and distributes it to the co-operative flax growers.

In its efforts to improve the quality of flax-fibre, Lnocentr has established a number of flax mills. At present the flax co-operatives control four factories for the preliminary working of flax, which have been erected by the contributions of Lnocentr and the local unions. Of these four works, two are tow factories and two flax-retting works. The annual capacity of these factories is about 1,200 tons of flax and 1,650 tons of tow, with a value of about 1,055,000 roubles.

As will be seen from the following table, the turnover of Lnocentr increases from year to year:

			Thousand of Roubles.	Per Cent.
1923-24	..	..	10,758·9	100·0
1924-25	..	..	25,152·1	233·7
1925-26	..	..	29,450·3	273·7
1926-27	..	..	35,603·0	330·0
1927-28	..	..	48,398·0	462·0

KHLEBOCENTR: ALL-RUSSIAN CENTRAL UNION OF GRAIN PRODUCERS CO-OPERATIVES.

The Central Union of Grain Producers, Khlebocentr, was formed on July 1, 1926, as the head organisation of the agricultural grain co-operatives, by the transference of grain operations from the sphere of the Selskosojus. Apart from grain Khlebocentr also deals in oilseed, (sunflower seed, etc.) and bean production. At the time of its formation—1926-27—the Khlebocentr included 76 local general purposes unions, 1,900 co-operatives, and 933,900 peasant households. By 1927-28, this had increased to 79 unions and about 2,000 co-operatives, which included a total of 950,000 peasant households. The specialisation of agricultural grain co-operatives is only now beginning. In 1928 a number of special grain co-operatives was organised. There were also established several local " railway station " groups of co-operatives belonging to the radius of a certain railway station. On October 1, 1928, there existed 519 co-operatives of this type chiefly in the predominantly grain-growing areas.

The grain deliveries effected through all the agricultural co-operative unions of U.S.S.R. are shown by the following figures:

1925-26	..	..	..	46,379,000 poods.
1926-27	..	..	..	97,133,000 ,,
1927-28	..	..	..	173,000,000 ,,

The grain collected by the agricultural primary co-operatives does not pass exclusively to the Central Union of Grain Producers. The grain destined for the supply of the home market is usually transmitted by the local unions direct to the consumers co-operatives, all the conditions under which this transference takes place being laid down in general agreements between the Khlebocentr and the Centrosojus (Central Union of Consumers Societies). In the same way, a certain proportion of the grain is collected by the primary co-operatives and delivered without recourse to the higher grades of organisation.

In 1928 Khlebocentr concluded contracts through the local co-operative organisations for sowing large areas of land. These contracts, made principally with various small peasant societies (collective farms, societies for joint use of agricultural machinery, societies for sowing), bind the peasants to deliver the contracted quantity of grain, reaching a certain standard of quality, and bind the co-operatives to make advances at stated times and to supply seeds and the means of production. In all contracts were concluded for 2·3 million hectares of spring corn and 3·15 million hectares of winter corn. Some of the contracts were entered into specially for sowing cleaned pure seeds. By means of these contracts Khlebocentr hopes to introduce improved methods of agriculture in peasant farming. A portion of the advances is made in kind (manure, seeds, implements). The poorer peasants receive larger advances. During the spring of 1929

Khlebocentr intends to make contracts for sowing 5·5 million hectares with spring corn.

The percentage participation of the agricultural co-operatives (including the Ukraine) in the total wheat collection of the U.S.S.R., amounted for 1925-26 to 28·9 per cent., for 1926-27 to 30·1 per cent. and for 1927-28 to 33 per cent., and in the first half of 1928-29 (July 1 to January 1) to 40 per cent. The sales operations of Khlebocentr on the home and foreign market have kept pace with this development in the collection of grain:

	Home Sales (in Poods).	Export.
1925-26[1]	34,373,000	13,056,000
1926-27	61,891,000	39,142,000

In 1927-28 and 1928-29 the export of Khlebocentr decreased to a very great extent owing to the general decrease of grain export in the U.S.S.R. Foreign sales are not effected through the foreign representatives of the agricultural co-operatives, but through the " Exportkhleb " Syndicate (Grain Export Co. Ltd.) in which the Khlebocentr is a partner.

Khlebocentr is also concerned with work on corn and grain culture. Its organisation includes industrial concerns, of which Khlebocentr itself controls some leased mills. The local unions own 71 concerns, with an average capacity of 16-50 tons in 24 hours. The total annual production of these concerns is about 5,700,000 double hundredweights, with a value of about 36 million roubles (1927).

The unions and co-operatives affiliated to the

[1] The agricultural year is calculated |from July 1 to July 1 by organisations dealing in grain.

48

Khlebocentr controlled on January 1, 1928, over 3,475 elevators, mostly in the centre of the collecting district, with a capacity of 1,500,000 tons. In addition, Khlebocentr makes use of the elevators of the state grain organisations.

In 1928 Khlebocentr already occupied a very important position as a grain collecting and marketing organisation, and began making great strides in furthering the development of peasant grain agriculture. One of the chief aims of Khlebocentr, together with Semenovodsojus, is to introduce, instead of ordinary seeds, the best selected seeds, giving larger crops. Seed societies (affiliated to Semenovodsojus) are occupied with the production of improved seeds, and Khlebocentr introduces them to the peasants and purchases all crops grown from such seeds. The seed unions cultivated in the year 1926, 195,700 hectares of land and in 1927, 433,300 hectares for the production of selected seeds. Apart from this, Khlebocentr gets improved selected seeds from the special Government stock established for this purpose. The task of increasing average crops for a unit of land confronts Khlebocentr in all its magnitude and requires a series of practical measures which the Union puts into operation as far as resources for this purpose are available.

SOJUSKARTOFFEL: THE CENTRAL UNION OF POTATO GROWERS CO-OPERATIVES.

The Sojuskartoffel has as its sphere of operations a number of districts in the central industrial region, the districts of Kostroma and Jaroslav, the Central Black Earth District, the Western region and the Middle Volga district. Founded in 1921, the Sojuskartoffel found itself in direct touch with the primary

E

co-operatives and consequently closely linked to their members, the potato growers. The following table will illustrate phases in the development of the central union:

	1924.	1925.	1926.	1927.
Number of unions	16	14	16	15
Number of primary co-operatives ..	64	67	70	101
Number of members of primary co-operatives (thousands)	24·3	25·1	30·1	38·6

In the districts of Jaroslav and Kostroma, Sojuskartoffel relies entirely on specalised unions and societies dealing with potato processing and supplying the state industries with potatoes and their products. The principal work of the agricultural potato co-operatives is in the conversion of potatoes into starch, treacle and dextrin (starch gum). In 1926-27 the co-operative potato factories handled over 52 per cent. of the potatoes used in the starch and treacle industry and produced over 55 per cent. of the total starch manufactured in the R.S.F.S.R. The potato co-operatives take the following share of the total output of final starch products in the R.S.F.S.R.:

1924-25	..	..	..	..	..	42·0
1925-26	..	..	..	..	..	48·0
1926-27	..	..	..	..	..	49·2

The output of products of the potato co-operatives through the Sojuskartoffel is shown by the following sale figures (in cwts.):

	Starch.	Treacle.	Potato Flour.	Total.	Per Cent.
1923-24	23,996·7	15,724·8	114·7	44,799·3	100
1924-25	72,612·6	37,723·2	3,030·3	113,366·1	253
1925-26	107,780·5	62,653·5	5,503·7	175,937·7	392·7
1926-27	140,000·0	145,000·0	9,000·0	302,090·0	697·0

In 1928 the local unions and primary co-operatives owned 113 potato-grating factories, 41 starch-drying depots, 7 treacle factories and 3 potato-flour and dextrin factories—a total of 164 establishments. Of these, 108 are the property of Sojuskartoffel. The foundation capital of all these undertakings amounts to over 10 million roubles.

CENTROTABAKSOJUS: CENTRAL UNION OF TOBACCO CO-OPERATIVES.

The Centrotabaksojus was formed in January, 1926, by the removal of tobacco operations from the activities of the Selskosojus, and acts as head organisation for the system of tobacco co-operatives. Its sphere of action includes the districts of light tobacco growing in the U.S.S.R., the autonomous Republic of the Crimea, Abkhaszka, the Black Sea littoral and the North Caucasus, and also the Mahorka-growing districts in the R.S.F.S.R. (Tambov, Voronesh, Pensa and the autonomous Republic of the Volga Germans).

The operations of Centrotabaksojus are divided into two main organisational groups corresponding with these two spheres of activity: (1) co-operatives of the light tobacco region and (2) co-operatives of the Mahorka region.

The following table is descriptive of the organisation:

April 1, 1928.	Number of Unions.	Number of Co-operatives: Special.	Number of Co-operatives: General.	Number of Co-operative Growers (Thousands).
Light tobacco	7	75 }	501	{ 33·9
Mahorka ..	5	54 }		{ 16·8

AGRICULTURAL CO-OPERATION

While the co-operative unions in the light tobacco region are almost entirely specialised, the general purposes unions predominate in the region of Mahorka plantation, as, in contrast to light tobacco culture, the planting of Mahorka is not a main crop but is only planted by the peasants alongside other field crops.

The turnover of Centrotabaksojus, together with Silgospodar (Ukraine) and the Transcaucasian agricultural co-operatives, is expressed in the following figures:

	1926-27.	1927-28.
Light tobacco	19,815 tons	22,786 tons
Mahorka	99,278 ,,	78,509 ,,

This stands in the following percentage relationship to the total tobacco output of the Soviet Union:

	1925-26.	1926-27.	1927-28.
Tobacco	38·7	65·2	77·9
Mahorka	45·6	87·8	100·0

The bulk of this output passes to the State industries ("Tabak-Syrjo" and "Mahorka-Syndicat"), with which special agreements have been concluded. The local unions control three tobacco factories, one for the manufacture of light tobacco and the two others for Mahorka. One of these factories belongs to the central union, while the two others are leased. The capacity of all factories is 3,200 poods of light tobacco and 225·300 boxes of Mahorka in 24 hours. The foundation capital of all factories is 130,000 roubles.

Tabaksojus exports part of its tobacco abroad. These exports amounted in 1926-27 to £78,000 and in 1927-28 to £89,180 in the U.S.S.R., not counting tobacco handed over by the local Unions to the State Organisations for export. The sale of exported tobacco was entrusted to the State Trade Organisations abroad and not to the representatives of the agricultural unions.

PLODOVINSOJUS: CENTRAL UNION OF FRUIT, VEGETABLE AND WINE GROWERS CO-OPERATIVES.

Plodovinsojus began its activities as head organisation of the fruit, vegetable and wine-growing agricultural co-operatives in November, 1924. The central union links up the peasants co-operative organisations engaged in these activities. Federation takes place through special co-operative unions of gardeners', vegetable and wine growers' co-operative societies and also agricultural credit co-operatives working in the same districts.

The sphere of operations of the Plodovinsojus includes the Crimea, and the North Caucasus region. Transcaucasia and the Middle Asiatic region are not included Plodovinsojus as members, but have special agreements with it.

The productive work of the fruit and vegetable co-operatives consists in drying fruit and vegetables. Plodovinsojus owns two productive works; the local unions control 43 factories, of which 32 are drying centres, 7 jam factories and 4 combined jam and drying establishments. The yearly capacity of all factories is 620,000 poods, and the value of the plant 319,000 roubles.

AGRICULTURAL CO-OPERATION

Amongst the central unions not yet mentioned, reference must be made to the " Sveklocentr " (Central Union of Beetroot Co-operatives) and the Cotton Bureau which do not carry on any active work, as the production of beet, as of cotton, is not handled on the market. Beet, which is principally transformed into sugar, will not bear long storage or transport, and consequently passes straight from the co-operative unions to the sugar factories.

In the same way, cotton is principally produced for the state industries and comes straight from the plantations to the state cotton-ginning works for the supply of the state weaving and spinning mills. Consequently, the central unions of beet and cotton growers do not organise their members for the disposal of their produce so much as for the systematic growing of these crops. The number of beet and cotton growers affiliated to the agricultural co-operative system increases from year to year, and reached the following figures in 1926-27:

Agricultural Beet Growers Co-operatives.

Number of unions	19
Number of primary co-operatives	321
Number of growers affiliated to co-operatives (thousands) ..	83·7

Cotton Growers Co-operatives.

Number of unions	24
Number of primary co-operatives	707
Number of co-operative households which are engaged in cotton growing (percentage)	92

Special agreements are entered into between the growers and the corresponding co-operatives on the basis of a stated sown acreage, for the supply of beet to the sugar factories and cotton to the ginning works. If the growers lack the means of production, these are supplied by the co-operatives, either in money or goods. The co-operatives undertake to settle all such accounts

54

with the growers and bear full responsibility to the Unions in this respect, the latter being responsible in turn to the Central Union for the money spent.

This system of contracts ensures a sufficient supply of raw material to the sugar and cotton industries, and also supplies the peasants with an incentive to increased production. At the same time, the co-operatives are sure of systematic and uniform work.

The percentage of contracted areas to the total sown acreage is as follows:

					Sugar-Beet.	Cotton.
1924-25 ..	..	..	..	..	35	58·9
1925-26 ..	..	..	..	..	48·2	75
1926-27 ..	..	..	..	..	81·2	89
1927-28 ..	..	..	..	..	83·7	95

Semenovodsojus unites the peasant co-operatives which deal with the production of improved selected seeds. In many districts whole colonies of peasants are occupied with this work. On April 1, 1928, there were 2,911 seed-growing societies. A portion of the seeds necessary for reproduction is imported by Semenovodsojus (formerly Selskosojus) from abroad. In 1926-27 the imports amounted to £110,000, in 1927-28 to £100,000. Seeds produced by the seed-growing societies are sold by Semenovodsojus to special centres (Khlebocentr, Lnocentr) for sowing large areas.

Pchelovodsojus unites special beekeepers co-operative societies. The object of Pchelovodsojus is to dispose of the honey produced by the apicultural co-operatives on the central markets and abroad. In 1927-28 Pchelovodsojus exported 340 tons of honey.

Knigosojus is a special publishing centre, which publishes and distributes co-operative and agricultural literature amongst the peasantry. It also issues forms for accountancy, necessary for the agricultural co-operatives, and further supplies the peasant population with wireless sets and accessories.

Koopstrakhsojus insures the property of the agricultural co-operatives and unions. The individual insurance of separate peasant farms is effected by the State Insurance organisation.

It is anticipated that in 1929 the following Central Unions will be organised: (1) horse-breeding; (2) sheep-breeding (neither of which are associated with Zhivotnovodsojus); (3) technical culture (Kenaf, Kendir—plants from which different kinds of textile fibres are produced).

V. THE CO-OPERATIVE ORGANISATION OF PEASANT ECONOMY

The work which the agricultural co-operatives are carrying on in the Soviet Union for the technical improvement of agriculture are to a large extent bound up with the promotion in agriculture of different kinds of collective farming co-operative societies.

Visualising the widely scattered peasant villages and holdings divided from one another by whole country-sides, which make it almost impossible to arrange the common use of heavy machinery, increase the difficulty of any fundamental work of improvement and hinder the introduction of improved seeds, considering further the dominance of individual interests amongst small producers, it will be apparent that the transition to a higher level of agricultural production will be attended by extreme difficulties.

After the agricultural co-operatives had begun their work with the organisation of the output, the supply of agricultural requirements and credit—that is with the improvement of processes connected with the marketing of the peasant—they gradually took over the organisation and improvement of agricultural production itself. The forms of this activity are extraordinarily various and are adapted to the practical requirements of each region.

The simplest productive "collectives" established for joint purchase and joint use of heavy agricultural machinery, pedigree stock and selected seeds entered on a wider development. Improvement co-operatives exist in considerable numbers, and occupy themselves with the communal drainage and irrigation of newly cultivated lands. On April 1, 1928, the following productive collectives were in existence:[1]

Tractor and machinery co-operatives	17,989
Cattle-breeding co-operatives	3,838
Stock-breeding and cow-testing co-operatives ..	310
Improvement co-operatives	5,467
Seed-growing co-operatives	2,911
Other simple associations	1,266

As examples of associations exhibiting a profoundly collective form, in which the peasant is no longer an individual producer, there are the collective groups ("Kolkhos") which may be classified in three types, according to the degree in which the processes of production have been rendered collective:

1. Co-operatives for communal working of the land.

2. Agricultural artels.

3. Agricultural communes.

The last named is the only type of collective where the private ownership of the means of production has completely ceased to exist, and all work is carried out

[1] "Wild" co-operatives not included.

on a socialist basis. Collective groups are often formed directly by transformation of individual households into collective farming associations. Still more often they are formed by a development of the simple productive associations (machinery associations, improvement associations), which carries the peasant along step by step. On the other hand, there also occurs a development of special co-operatives (dairying, potato, poultry) concerned with the disposal of agricultural products, by which they gradually turn to communal tilling of the soil, or become agricultural artels and so assume the form of collective groups, or Kolkhos.

On April 1, 1928, there were 29,887 Kolkhos of all kinds in the Union, of which 20,054 were co-operatives for the communal working of the soil, 7,173 artels and 2,660 communes.

The increase in the number of the collective farms and the primary productive societies is more rapid than that of the credit societies and special trading co-operatives. Amongst the collective farms, the growth of the societies for the common use of agricultural machinery and cultivation of land is more rapid than that of the communes. From 1928 the Kolkhos have begun to play an important part in agriculture. From July 1 to November 1, 20 million poods of grain were sold by them to the Unions. Their average crop per unit of land in 1928 was greater by 25 per cent. than that of the individual peasants.

The organisation of productive co-operatives serves the peasant by making it possible for him not only to employ machinery, tractors, pedigree stock and selected seeds, but also considerably to increase his crop yield and milk yield and the quality of his agricultural produce. It is to this circumstance that must be attributed the rapid development of the co-operative organisation of production in agriculture.

Simultaneously with the organisation of productive co-operative societies of various kinds, the technical agricultural work of the general purposes and also the specialised agricultural unions developed further. The erection of various agricultural and productive concerns was usually closely connected with the general sales and supply activities of the central and local unions.

In their technical agricultural work, the agricultural co-operatives occupy themselves with the technical reconstruction of peasant economy, with its promotion on more intensive lines, with an increase in output, an improvement in the quality of agricultural produce and in general with the raising of the cultural level of the co-operative members. On October 1, 1927, there were 20,332 undertakings of different kinds in existence which are grouped as follows:

Grain-cleaning stations	7,470
Hiring depots of agricultural machinery	4,500
Stud farms	5,362
Various (breeding stations, gardens, breeding associations, etc.)	3,000

The number of agronomists at the disposal of co-operative members and maintained by the agricultural co-operatives stands at about 3,000. Of the total of available machines at the disposal of the members of co-operative societies and other institutions, and of the depots belonging to the local land organisations, the agricultural co-operatives own 55 per cent. of the sowing machines, 48 per cent. of the seed-cleaning machines and 59 per cent. of the remaining machinery (1926-27).

Productive works for the processing of agricultural produce belonging to the agricultural co-operatives, which are members of the Union of Unions, number, according to current computation, about 17,000.

These may be divided according to their individual branch of industry as follows:

Creameries, cheese factories, butter factories (belonging to Maslocentr)	7,696
Treacle, starch, and other potato-working factories ..	164
Steam, water, and grist mills	2,700
Various concerns of factory type, also workshops	6,400
Total	16,960

For 1927-28 a scheme of reconstruction was drawn up and the requirements for the construction of co-operative buildings for the processing and warehousing of agricultural products was estimated at 28,962,000 roubles. Concerns will be newly established in the following branches of industry: 1,195 in the dairy industry, 98 in the poultry industry, 64 in the cattle industry (meat, sinews, etc.), 84 in the grain industry (elevators, mills, granaries), and 17 in the potato industry. According to the information for nine months this plan has been carried out in full.

The activities of the agricultural co-operatives, in all their variety, aim at the unification of the scattered peasant farms and at the raising of their technical standard on the basis of unified labour. All the fundamental activities of the co-operatives in one way or another support this object.

Credits granted for obtaining machinery, seeds, animals; organisation of manufacture and disposal of products; supply of agricultural implements; contracts for sowing; the work of tractor colonies and hiring stations, breeding stations and stations for cleaning seeds; primary productive societies; finally, collective farms (as a means of uniting labour and the means of production) and communes (where all labour is equally divided)—all these forms of activity, being in themselves a means of raising the standard of peasant farming, lead to greatly increased and unified agricultural production. In so far as capitalistic farming is excluded under the conditions of the U.S.S.R., collective farming is the only possible form of farming on a big scale. It is also the only way to replace the old-fashioned small farms by the modern mechanised technique of highly productive farming.

VI. THE FINANCIAL POSITION OF THE AGRICULTURAL CO-OPERATIVES

The financial position of the agricultural co-operatives can be learnt from the balance sheets of the local co-operatives, the unions and the central unions. The balance of the whole movement has grown steadily. On October 1, 1925, this stood at 795.3 million roubles, and on October 1, 1926, at 1,000.8 millions, on October 1, 1927, at 1,554.6 millions, and on April 1, 1928, 2,200 millions. This development has not occurred uniformly in all grades of the system. The balance of the local co-operatives has risen from 376.3 on October 1, 1925, to 747.8 million roubles on October 1, 1927 (about 1,000 millions on April 1, 1928), that of the co-operative unions from 244.8 to 517.8 (850.0 on April 1, 1928), and that of the central unions from 129.8 to 199.3 million roubles (350 on April 1, 1928). The resources of the co-operative movement rose in the period from October 1, 1925, to October 1, 1927, from 175 to 344 million roubles, that is 98 per cent. The resources of the local co-operatives stood at 202 million roubles on October 1, 1927. The profits reached a total of 21 millions in the year 1926-27 as against 16.6 millions in the previous year. In the local co-operatives the accumulation of resources owned by the society proceeds more rapidly than the growth of external resources. Between October 1, 1925, and October 1, 1927, share capital in reserve increased 96 per cent., and in the same period, loan capital increased 88 per cent. In the unions, both general purposes and special, the growth of capital has followed the same lines as in the local co-operatives. By October 1, 1927, the local unions had raised their capital to 78 million roubles, thus securing an increase in capital more than equal to that in the unions' general balance.

The general and trading costs in 1924-25 amounted to 12·4 per cent. of the turnover, but were decreased by 9 per cent. in 1926-27. It must be observed that the financial strength is not the same in the various general purposes unions, and that this financial position corresponds to the general economic conditions of the regions concerned. The strongest unions financially are those in whose area the peasants have achieved a high output of goods. The balance of the central unions (excluding Knigosojus, Strachsojus and Vsekoles) rose in the last two years from October 1, 1925, to October 1, 1927, from 129.8 million roubles to 199.3 millions. The capital of these central unions stood at 24 millions on October 1, 1925, and at 32 millions on October 1, 1927. The profits of the whole co-operative movement stood at 13.6 millions in 1924-25, at 17.5 millions in 1925-26 and at 26.5 millions in 1926-27.

The figures given above regarding the financial position of the agricultural co-operatives, lead to the conclusion that in spite of the large capital in the hands of agricultural co-operatives which considerably exceeds 300 million roubles, this is not sufficient. The three million turnover of the co-operative movement, its extending organisation and the accelerated development of the individual societies, must be taken into consideration. On these grounds, the agricultural co-operative societies are compelled to work to a large extent on credit and to be perpetually considering ways of obtaining support from their members and raising the amount of contributions and investments. These efforts are gradually bearing fruit, as may be seen from the above figures, which show capital increasing more rapidly than loans. A generally satisfactory solution now depends on the improvement and increased productivity of the land.

VII. THE FOREIGN TRADE OF THE AGRICULTURAL CO-OPERATIVES

The external trade of the agricultural central unions is adjusted to the requirements of the peasants. It consists in the export of agricultural produce such as grain, butter, eggs, poultry, hides and skins, tobacco, fruit, flax, etc., and in the import of the means of peasant production such as agricultural machinery and tools, fittings, metals, manures, seeds and cattle. The central co-operative unions have received the state concession of independent entry on the foreign market; import and export operations are carried on through the foreign representatives of the co-operatives within the limit of the general law of the U.S.S.R. on foreign trade, that is to say, carried on independently but under the supervision of the Soviet trade delegations abroad. The central unions have foreign representatives in London, Berlin, New York, Paris and Riga which exist abroad as legally constituted joint stock companies with limited liability (those in Riga and Paris are branches of the London Company). The shareholders in these companies are the co-operative central unions.[1] The turnover in foreign trade of the central unions of agricultural co-operatives has stood as follows in recent years:

			Total Turnover in Pounds.
1923-24 ..	..	..	.. 2,382,000
1924-25 ..	..	..	.. 6,207,000
1925-26 ..	..	..	.. 7,541,000
1926-27 ..	..	..	.. 9,712,000
1927-28 ..	..	..	.. 8,429,000

The decrease in the turnover in 1927-28, which was due to the falling off of grain export, was made up for to a great extent by other products.

Of the total turnover in the last five years £34,271,000 represented £29,755,000 exports and £4,516,000 imports. Sales and purchases take place principally in Germany, America, England, Austria, Czechoslovakia and Sweden. Trade has developed to a small extent in France, Denmark and the Baltic countries. The different types of business are distributed amongst individual countries as follows:

America.—Purchase of tractors, mowing machines, binder twine; sale of furs, poultry and game.

Germany.—Purchase of agricultural machinery and tools, creamery appliances, flax and potato working plant, minor agricultural requirements, seeds, barrel staves, artificial manures, chemicals; sale of butter, eggs, poultry, furs and raw hides, flax, grain and tobacco, honey.

England.—Sale of grain, butter, eggs, poultry, flax, furs, bristles, casings, fruit, and honey; purchase of metals, threshing machines, seeds, saws, minor agricul-

---

[1] Including Vsekoles.

tural appliances, binder twine, pedigree cattle, sheep, pigs and poultry.

Sweden.—Purchase of separators, seeds, artificial manures, and horses.

Austria.—Purchase of scythes, seed-cleaning and threshing machines.

Czechoslovakia.—Purchase of ploughs and other implements.

Denmark.—Purchase of barrel staves, dairy appliances, seeds; sale of butter.

France.—Sale of flax, hemp, eggs, poultry, furs and grain; purchase of agricultural appliances and seeds.

Latvia.—Purchase of seeds, manures, pedigree cattle, minor appliances; sale of butter, eggs and furs.

The whole foreign trade of the agricultural co-operatives is not effected through their foreign representatives; in a few cases, particularly in the sale of grain and flax, other foreign organisations take part and undertake sales on a commission basis. For the export of grain all the grain organisations of the Soviet Union are united in the general exporting syndicate " Exportkhleb," which undertakes the sale of all exported grain. The agricultural co-operatives, with their head organisation, the " Khlebocentr," are members of this syndicate. A flax export syndicate, " Exportlen," for the sale of flax abroad has recently been formed and handled the entire export trade of flax and hemp. In this syndicate the agricultural co-operatives represented by the " Lnocentr " as principal partner have a predominant influence.

It must be observed further that the agricultural co-operatives of the Ukraine, federated in the " Silksi Gospodar," also have jointly with the Ukrainian Consumers Societies their independent representation in Germany and England, through which they carry on foreign trade. In America " Silksi Gospodar " works through the New York representatives of the agricultural co-operatives, Selskosojus, Inc.

IMPORT.

The supply of the peasants with the means of production, which is effected for the most part through Selskosojus, takes place on the one hand through the steadily growing home industry, and on the other through import from abroad.

The industrialisation and intensification of agriculture to which the Soviet Union is devoting peculiar attention, makes the supplies of special importance. The backwardness of the peasants and the consequent need to increase output and make agriculture collective, calls for a mass supply of agriculture with tractors, agricultural machines and implements, manures, graded seeds, means of combating pests, etc. The development of importing by the agricultural co-operatives[1] in the last five years may be seen in the following figures:

					Pounds.	Per Cent.
1923-24	..	..	..	..	133,298	100
1924-25	..	..	..	..	1,053,805	790·4
1925-26	..	..	..	..	1,136,870	855·5
1926-27	..	..	..	..	1,156,871	867·7
1927-28	..	..	..	..	1,035,600	831·6

It was already mentioned above that the slow development of imports is due to the steady expansion of the home industry of the U.S.S.R. Further, a gradual change in the character of the imports has taken place in

[1] Excluding the Ukraine.

66

so far as there has been a change-over from the import of the simpler agricultural machines and implements to the import of complicated machinery such as tractors, mowing machines, etc., representing a type of purchase of special significance for the industrialisation and collective organisation of agriculture. The following observations must be made with regard to individual articles.

Tractors.—Up to 1914 the number of tractors in Russia was 187, of which 72 were fitted with steam and 115 with petrol-driven motors. In 1917 the number of tractors rose to 1,500. In 1921 the Union possessed 1,383 tractors (56 different types), of which only 444 were in use. All these tractors came from abroad. After the Revolution the import of tractors was as follows: 1922-23, 1,000; 1923-24, 1,500; 1924-25, 8,575; and 1926-27, 10,438. The agricultural co-operatives began importing tractors in 1922, but this import only reached a considerable figure in 1924. The principal orders went to America, and amounted to almost the whole import—602 tractors in 1924, 1,100 in 1925, 2,497 in 1926. In 1927, 1,449 tractors were imported from America. All tractors were provided with complete fittings. In 1927, 200 tractors of the W.D. type (Hanomag) were purchased experimentally in Germany. It will only be possible to say what prospects there are of an increased import of German tractors when the German and American tractors have been tested side by side. The agricultural co-operatives are the principal purchasers of tractors, because, owing to the system of land distribution in the Soviet Union, the use of tractors is practically confined to the collective peasants' associations and the tractor co-operatives within the agricultural co-operative movement.

The import of *agricultural machinery and implements and the minor agricultural requirements* amounted in the past four years to about £3,000,000. Of this total about £2,200,000 represented the import of tractors and agricultural machinery, and about £800,000 that of various agricultural requirements, appliances and tools. Of the larger agricultural machines, harvesters and combined threshing machines were purchased in America, Germany and the United Kingdom; these, like the tractors, are principally in use by the collective associations and machine co-operatives. Seed cleaners are bought in Austria. The majority of mowing machines are made principally in America and Germany. Now, however, the home industry is turning out mowing machines of satisfactory quality and acceptable price, no development of imports from abroad is likely to take place. Ploughs are purchased principally in Germany (67·1 per cent.) and also in Czechoslovakia. Separators and dairying appliances are widely distributed in the Soviet Union. In the last four years separators to the value of about £300,000 were manufactured by Selskosojus and Maslocentr. Latterly, too, the separators manufactured by the Permer Separator Works (in the Ural) have reached a considerable output. Separators are bought almost exclusively in Sweden, and dairy fittings in Denmark, Germany and Sweden.

The import of creamery appliances began in 1926; in 1926-27 the import from Germany amounted to £50,000. The creamery appliances coming from abroad gave the impulse to the construction of large and well built and equipped creameries in the domain of industrialised butter production. In addition, a large number of barrel staves, amounting in yearly value to over £40,000, were purchased abroad for use in the export of butter. Amongst other imports of agricultural machinery and implements into the Soviet Union, mention must be made of the purchase at an early stage of machinery for working flax. Minor agricultural requirements are purchased in various countries; for instance, in the last three years about 1,500,000 scythes have been imported from Austria. Binder twine is bought in America, England and Germany. The demand is for over 2,000 tons yearly. Cross saws and files were bought in England up to £30,000 per annum. Iron pitchforks were imported to the number of a million in 1926-27. Besides machinery and tools, the agricultural co-operatives also import seeds on a large scale. The purchase of seeds is carried on in a large number of countries—Germany, England, France, Denmark, Sweden, Czechoslovakia and Latvia. In

	Classification by Countries in per Cent.	
	1926-27.	1927-28.
America	40·5	57·0
Germany	30·0	25·9
England	7·6	7·9
Other countries	21·9	19·2

	Classification by Type of Goods in per Cent.	
	1926-27.	1927-28.
Tractors, tractor ploughs, spare parts and machinery	56·3	71·1
Implements and appliances	4·3	—
Seeds..	11·9	6·8
Chemicals	3·8	4·7
Dairy appliances, separators, and barrel staves	9·6	37·3
Various	14·1	9·8
Total	100·0	100·0

the last four years seeds to a total value of £560,000 were imported. Without going into details of those goods which are only imported to a small extent, the table on page 69 gives the constituents of the import by agricultural co-operative societies according to countries and types of imported goods.

EXPORT.

The fundamental products of the land, such as grain, butter, flax, eggs, poultry and hides, which account for 95 per cent. of the total export of the agricultural co-operatives, go principally to England, and Germany. A short account follows of the exporting activities of the agricultural co-operative central unions with regard to individual commodities.

Butter.

The local dairying co-operatives and artels cover nine-tenths of the entire milk industry. The dairying co-operatives have developed with peculiar intensity in the area of " Butter Export "—West Siberia and the Urals. The export of co-operative butter began long before the Revolution. Already in 1911 the Siberian Creameries Artel Union exported great quantities of butter abroad. The infinite wealth of fertile meadows and abundance of natural food for cattle gave Siberian butter a European reputation for its natural qualities, low water content and high vitamin character. Dairy farming in the Soviet Union developed rapidly, and the total cattle population in 1927 exceeded that of the pre-war period by 13 per cent. Consequently, in spite of the increased home consumption (which in the country has doubled and in the principal towns has trebled since before the war), Butter Export has great prospects of success. The export trade of the dairying co-operatives through their central Union, " Maslocentr," has developed in the last few years as follows:

1924-25	..	..	..	..	108,705 double tons of butter.
1925-26	..	..	..	..	119,825 ,, ,, ,,
1926-27	..	..	..	..	180,197 ,, ,, ,,
1927-28	..	..	..	..	186,011 ,, ,, ,,

Maslocentr is the principal exporter of butter and takes the following place amongst the other exporters of butter in the Soviet Union: 1925-26, 5·61 per cent.; 1926-27, 65 per cent.; 1927-28, 69·3 per cent. The principal markets for Siberian butter are England and Germany. Smaller quantities are also sold to Denmark, Norway, Holland, America and France. Maslocentr is continuously engaged on thorough measures for the qualitative improvement of butter. These measures have already given good results, and, in the judgment of the Western European trade press and well-known business men, the quality of Siberia and Ural butter has so far improved in the last two years that the butter sold by Maslocentr—known in Western Europe under the " Lebedj " (Swan) mark—has gradually won the recognition of the market. The technical backwardness of Russian dairying, its great distance from its markets, have nevertheless an unfavourable influence on the quality of the butter, but the growing perfection of the industry, the introduction of scientific feeding, the improvement of breeds and other measures, including the building of cold stores and the speeding up of transport, are finally leading to the removal of these shortcomings, so that the qualities of Siberian butter may receive full recognition.

AGRICULTURAL CO-OPERATION

Egg and Poultry Export.

Much importance is assigned to the export of eggs and poultry. In the pre-war period the export of eggs reached in the 1913 standard of value a total of 90 million roubles or 6 per cent. in value of the total exports. Before the Revolution the collection and dispatch of poultry produce was principally in the hands of foreign exporters, who regarded their employment as temporary and consequently would not invest a considerable capital for any length of time. In the last years before the war a few small Russian firms, often single persons, took part in the export of eggs formerly carried on by foreign exporters, and consequently had the opportunity of learning the egg and poultry export trade. The reorganisation of the egg export after the war and the Revolution first began in 1923, when a number of organisations were formed for the collection and export of eggs.

The value of poultry produce exported from the Union stood in 1923-24 at 10 million roubles, 1924-25 at 31 millions, 1925-26 at 27 millions, and 1926-27 at 40 millions. In the 1926-27 period the export of eggs amounted to 6,000 truck loads. The agricultural co-operatives, represented by the Ptizevodsojus, first came into the foreign market in 1926. The growth of the exports of Ptizevodsojus may be illustrated by the following figures: 1925-26, 240 truck loads of eggs; 1926-27, 1,154 truck loads; 1927-28, 1,870 truck loads. The percentage relation of the Ptizevodsojus to the egg exporters of the R.S.F.S.R. was 19·7 per cent. in 1925-26, 37·7 per cent. in 1926-27, and 41·7 per cent. in 1927-28. In the Ukraine the percentage of the egg export handled by the " Kooptach " is much more striking. The co-operative movement of the Ukraine

covers the greater part of the egg collection. Ptizevodsojus disposes of its produce in Germany and England, and to some extent also in Latvia and France.
Germany takes the first place. In the last two years
the export of eggs (per cent.) has been as follows:

	1926.	1927.
England	37·0	32·1
Germany	61·2	47·9
Latvia	1·8	12·1
France	—	7·9

The goods of Ptizevodsojus have the trade-mark " P.S."

Furs and Skins.

Russian furs have always been one of the most
important articles of export; the principal buying
countries are Germany and England. After the Revolution Russian furs appeared once more on the world
market, and their value in 1925-26 reached 72 million
roubles, and in 1926-27, 86 millions. Before the war
agricultural co-operatives took no part in the export
of furs. They first took up the collection and export
of these valuable articles in 1923, through the Selskosojus, and later through a special central union, the
Zhivotnovodsojus. In the last few years Zhivotnovodsojus has exported furs and raw hides to the following
values: 6,080,000 roubles in 1926-27 and 9,291,000
roubles in 1927-28. Furs are exported to England,
Germany and America. In 1927 the export to England
was 66 per cent., to Germany 30·6 per cent., and to
other countries 3·4 per cent. Since 1926-27, after
Germany once more took a leading place as a market
for furs, their export by Zhivotnovodsojus to Leipzig
has steadily increased.

AGRICULTURAL CO-OPERATION

Bacon.

Zhivotnovodsojus (in U.S.S.R.) has to do with the export of bacon as have also the Ukrainian Agricultural Co-operatives. Zhivotnovodsojus has bacon factories in Pokrovsk and Voronesh. Their bacon is sold principally in England. The improvement in bacon, as also its export, is increasing rapidly: in 1926/27 Zhivotnovodsojus exported only 346 tons, whereas in 1927/28 the export of bacon amounted to 1,481 tons. The rapid breeding of bacon-type pigs and the building of new factories (Viatka, Krasnodar) tend to a further increase in the export of bacon.

Flax.

It is well known that the export of Russian flax in the pre-war period amounted to over 85 per cent. of the total world export, being equal to about 300,000 tons. After the Revolution Russian flax was one of the first products which found its way to the foreign market, though in greatly reduced bulk. This was owing to the decline in agriculture and the separation from the U.S.S.R. of some of the important flax-growing areas (Latvia, Estonia). At present the bodies engaged in flax export are in part the state organisations and the consumers' co-operatives with the Centrosojus, but to a larger extent the agricultural co-operatives represented by the Lnocentr, the successor of the former Central Union of flax-growers co-operatives. Lnocentr is in active business communication with leading foreign flax firms, and takes the first place amongst the other exporters of the Soviet Union. The Lnocentr owes the extension of its operations and the good results of its marketing to its painstaking care in grading the flax and its accurate attention to orders from abroad. In the last three years the flax export of Lnocentr has developed as follows:

1924-25	..	..	..	..	13,173·7 tons.
1925-26	..	..	..	..	20,819·9 ,,
1926-27	..	..	..	..	15,229·5 ,,
1927-28	..	..	..	..	14,045·0 ,,

The percentage relationship of the Lnocentr to the other flax producers of the U.S.S.R. stood in 1924-25 at 23·3 per cent. and in 1925-26 at 28·1 per cent.; in 1926-27 at 41·0 per cent. and 1927-28 at 53 per cent.

In its efforts to secure flax of the highest quality, the Lnocentr carries on active agro-technical work, supplying the peasants with chemical manures, selected seeds, etc., and thus induces an increase in the planted acreage and a qualitative improvement in the yield. These measures will undoubtedly bring good results in the next few years and will compensate for the losses which Russian flax growers have suffered during the war and which have not yet been made good. An increase in the yield, which is still on a fairly low level, would also lead to an increased export of flax through the agricultural co-operatives. The sale of flax belonging to Lnocentr on the foreign market is undertaken by a special syndicate, "Exportlen," with sales depots abroad. It remains under the perpetual supervision of the agricultural co-operatives which are amongst the chief suppliers of flax.

The export of the remaining agricultural products does not take an important place in the general export of the agricultural co-operatives, and amounts to not more than 5 per cent. of the total exports of the agricultural co-operatives. It is an undoubted conclusion, however, that with the general growth of agriculture, produce which at present is only exported in small quantities, such as honey, fruit, tobacco, meat, pig-products, will form a considerable part of the export. In 1927-28 the agricultural co-operatives exported several million roubles worth of tobacco, bacon, honey, starch, sugar, resin, etc. The principal articles, however, are still (apart from grain and flax) butter, eggs, poultry and furs. In the export of grain, the agricultural co-operatives are the principal supplying organisations. As in the case of flax, the whole grain export is concentrated in the hands of a special export syndicate, to which the agricultural co-operatives supply and which handles their sales. The state has conferred on the grain export syndicate the sole right of sale on the foreign markets. The export of oil seeds is also in the hands of the same syndicate.

VIII. THE REPRESENTATION ABROAD OF THE AGRICULTURAL CO-OPERATIVES OF THE SOVIET UNION

As has been pointed out above, the foreign trade of the agricultural co-operatives takes place through their foreign representatives in London, Berlin, New York, Paris and Riga, with branches in Hamburg, Leipzig and Hull. The independent trade of the agricultural co-operatives on the foreign market began in 1923. In this year also, representatives were installed in London, Berlin and Riga. Other agencies were established somewhat later—New York at the beginning of 1924 and Paris at the end of the same year. The principal operations are carried on in London, Berlin and New York. The scope and character of the work of individual agencies is described below.

BERLIN AGENCY: SELSKOSOJUS G.M.B.H. BERLIN.

The sphere of action of this agency includes, outside Germany, also Austria, Czechoslovakia, Denmark, Holland, Norway and Sweden. These countries are the principal source of agricultural machinery and implements, seeds, manures, all kinds of agricultural and dairying appliances, flax manufacturing and creamery plant, butter-barrel staves, etc. Exports consist principally of butter, dressed hides and poultry produce. The total turnover of the Berlin agency may be seen from the following figures:[1]

	Total.	Per Cent.	Import.	Export.
1925	935,390	100	393,320	542,070
1926	1,384,326	148	466,285	918,041
1927	1,922,897	205·5	432,610	1,490,287
1927/28.. ..	2,464,300	264	440,000	2,024,300

The proportion of individual classes of goods sold through the Berlin Agency is shown by the first table on page 78.

The first place is taken by butter, which amounts to over one half of the total turnover. The expansion in the turnover of exported eggs is noteworthy, as it

[1] The companies representing the Agricultural Co-operatives abroad prepare their annual reports for the calendar year (ending January 1). As at the time of publication of this book reports for 1928 have not yet been issued, the following details are taken from the financial years October 1, 1927 to October 1, 1928, which will be quite sufficient for purposes of comparison with previous years.

has increased from 5·2 per cent. in 1925 to 24·6 per cent. in 1927/28. The turnover in furs also takes an important place.

	1925.		1926.		1927.		1927/28.	
	£	Per Cent.	£	Per Cent.	£	Per Cent.	£	Per Cent.
Butter	443,600	81·9	618.335	67·3	950,424	63·8	1,045,787	51·6
Eggs	28,200	5·2	101,702	11·1	344,647	23·1	497,330	24·6
Furs	60,400	11·1	151,700	16·5	158,889	10·7	324,589	16·0
Various (down, poultry, feathers, fruit, and vegetables)	9,870	1·8	46,304	5·1	36,325	2·4	156,594	7·8
Total	542,070	100·0	918,041	100·0	1,409,285	100·0	2,021,300	100·0

Although the export trade of the Berlin agency is confined to a comparatively small group of goods, the import trade is characterised by its complexity and by the multiplicity of goods imported. The principal purchasing customer of Selskosojus G.m.b.H. in Berlin is Selskosojus, Moscow. Important orders for creamery plant and dairying appliances are also undertaken for the Maslocentr. The turnover in imports for the last three years (in £) was as follows:

	1925.		1926.		1927.		1927/28.	
	£	Per Cent.	£	Per Cent.	£	Per Cent.	£	Per Cent.
Agricultural machinery, tractors, and tools ..	97,500	24·7	147,633	32·3	193,871	44·8	192,249	43·6
Agricultural appliances..	56,300	14·3	35,386	7·6	45,781	25·3		
Chemicals	14,250	3·6	27,798	5·9	22,076	5·1	49,162	11·2
Seeds	93,800	23·9	43,577	9·3	41,950	9·7	22,280	5·1
Barrel staves	40,400	10·3	43,260	9·3	24,782	5·7	—	
Machinery for flax and potato works	13,180	3·4	22,334	4·8	1,209	0·3	1,546	0·3
Wine-making appliances	12,500	3·2	6,008	1·3	8,401	1·9	14,989	3·4
Dairy apparatus ..	64,950	16·5	120,183	25·8	78,384	18·1	124,768	28·3
Various	440	0·1	20,106	4·3	15,992	7·2	35,613	8·1
Total ..	339,320	100·0	466,285	100·0	432,446	100·0	110,507	100·0

The most important turnover in imports was in agricultural machinery, tractors, tools, implements and

Simultaneously with the organisation of productive co-operative societies of various kinds, the technical agricultural work of the general purposes and also the specialised agricultural unions developed further. The erection of various agricultural and productive concerns was usually closely connected with the general sales and supply activities of the central and local unions.

In their technical agricultural work, the agricultural co-operatives occupy themselves with the technical reconstruction of peasant economy, with its promotion on more intensive lines, with an increase in output, an improvement in the quality of agricultural produce and in general with the raising of the cultural level of the co-operative members. On October 1, 1927, there were 20,332 undertakings of different kinds in existence which are grouped as follows:

Grain-cleaning stations	7,470
Hiring depots of agricultural machinery	4,500
Stud farms	5,362
Various (breeding stations, gardens, breeding associations, etc.)	3,000

The number of agronomists at the disposal of co-operative members and maintained by the agricultural co-operatives stands at about 3,000. Of the total of available machines at the disposal of the members of co-operative societies and other institutions, and of the depots belonging to the local land organisations, the agricultural co-operatives own 55 per cent. of the sowing machines, 48 per cent. of the seed-cleaning machines and 59 per cent. of the remaining machinery (1926-27).

Productive works for the processing of agricultural produce belonging to the agricultural co-operatives, which are members of the Union of Unions, number, according to current computation, about 17,000.

f goods accounted in 1925
27/28 for 43·6 per cent. of
ry appliances and barrel
/28 to the value of £124,767
cals to the value of £49,162
d goods are bought by the
ely direct, and only in excep-
ate trade organisations of the

formed itself into a limited
cording to German law and
in its trading activity. The
company amounts to 200,000
d by the various co-operative
elskosojus, Moscow, has a share
ntr 34,000 marks, Ptizevodsojus
and Selosojus, Ltd., London,
nainder is divided amongst the
Zhivotnovodsojus, Khlebocentr,
others. The orders from the
dled on a commission basis by
The commission serves to cover
ut orders. In relation to taxa-
milar commercial requirements,
acts like an ordinary German
ecutive power is in the hands of a
ho are nominated from a super-
lected by the general meeting.
H. has a branch in Hamburg
Leipzig. The Hamburg branch
s and poultry, the Leipzig branch

AGRICULTURAL CO-OPERATION

The London Agency: Selosojus, Ltd., London.

The activities of the London Agency are directed principally to the sale of exported goods, the financing of exports from the Soviet Union, and only to a limited extent to purchase. The principal sales take place in the following five articles: butter, eggs, poultry, bacon, furs and resin products. The imports are limited to threshing machines, saws, seeds, metals, pedigree cattle, sheep, pigs and poultry. In its structure Selosojus, Ltd., London, resembles Selskosojus G.m.b.H. and acts as an English limited company, the majority of whose shares are held by the co-operative organisations. Selosojus, Ltd., also acts as a commission house and receives a fixed commission for its services from its customers. The share capital consists of £75,000 (7,500 shares of £10 each). The majority of the shares are held by Selskosojus, Moscow (£31,160), Maslocentr (£26,370), Ptizevodsojus (£2,700) and Zhivotnovodsojus (£3,600). Selosojus has branches in Hull and Glasgow. The turnover of the London agency (without its Paris and Riga branches) has stood in the last three years as follows:

					£
1925	..	..	..	..	3,328,972
1926	..	..	..	..	3,208,644
1927	..	..	..	..	3,137,482
1927/28	..	..	..	..	3,330,700

In the last three years the turnover has remained about the same. Here must be recalled the special circumstances in which the London Agency found itself at the breaking off of diplomatic relations between England and the Soviet Union, which resulted in the almost complete cessation of purchases in England,

ided according to their individual
as follows:

ctories, butter factories (belonging	7,696
.. ..	164
other potato-working factories ..	2,700
ist mills	6,400
factory type, also workshops	
Total	16,960

cheme of reconstruction was drawn up
ients for the construction of co-opera-
r the processing and warehousing of
ducts was estimated at 28,962,000
ns will be newly established in the
hes of industry: 1,195 in the dairy
the poultry industry, 64 in the cattle
sinews, etc.), 84 in the grain industry
ls, granaries), and 17 in the potato
ording to the information for nine months
een carried out in full.
es of the agricultural co-operatives, in
y, aim at the unification of the scattered
s and at the raising of their technical
he basis of unified labour. All the funda-
ties of the co-operatives in one way or
ort this object.
anted for obtaining machinery, seeds,
anisation of manufacture and disposal of
pply of agricultural implements; contracts
the work of tractor colonies and hiring
eeding stations and stations for cleaning
ary productive societies; finally, collective
ary means of uniting labour and the means of
) and communes (where all labour is equally
ll these forms of activity, being in them-
ans of raising the standard of peasant farm-
:o greatly increased and unified agricultural

ment of the individual societies, must be taken into consideration. On these grounds, the agricultural co-operative societies are compelled to work to a large extent on credit and to be perpetually considering ways of obtaining support from their members and raising the amount of contributions and investments. These efforts are gradually bearing fruit, as may be seen from the above figures, which show capital increasing more rapidly than loans. A generally satisfactory solution now depends on the improvement and increased productivity of the land.

VII. THE FOREIGN TRADE OF THE AGRICULTURAL CO-OPERATIVES

The external trade of the agricultural central unions is adjusted to the requirements of the peasants. It consists in the export of agricultural produce such as grain, butter, eggs, poultry, hides and skins, tobacco, fruit, flax, etc., and in the import of the means of peasant production such as agricultural machinery and tools, fittings, metals, manures, seeds and cattle. The central co-operative unions have received the state concession of independent entry on the foreign market; import and export operations are carried on through the foreign representatives of the co-operatives within the limit of the general law of the U.S.S.R. on foreign trade, that is to say, carried on independently but under the supervision of the Soviet trade delegations abroad. The central unions have foreign representatives in London, Berlin, New York, Paris and Riga which exist abroad as legally constituted joint stock companies with limited liability (those in Riga and Paris are branches of the London Company). The shareholders in these companies are the co-operative central unions.[1] The turnover in foreign trade of the central unions of agricultural co-operatives has stood as follows in recent years:

			Total Turnover in Pounds.
1923-24 ..	..	..	.. 2,382,000
1924-25 ..	..	..	.. 6,207,000
1925-26 ..	..	..	.. 7,541,000
1926-27 ..	..	..	.. 9,712,000
1927-28 ..	..	..	.. 8,429,000

The decrease in the turnover in 1927-28, which was due to the falling off of grain export, was made up for to a great extent by other products.

Of the total turnover in the last five years £34,271,000 represented £29,755,000 exports and £4,516,000 imports. Sales and purchases take place principally in Germany, America, England, Austria, Czechoslovakia and Sweden. Trade has developed to a small extent in France, Denmark and the Baltic countries. The different types of business are distributed amongst individual countries as follows:

America.—Purchase of tractors, mowing machines, binder twine; sale of furs, poultry and game.

Germany.—Purchase of agricultural machinery and tools, creamery appliances, flax and potato working plant, minor agricultural requirements, seeds, barrel staves, artificial manures, chemicals; sale of butter, eggs, poultry, furs and raw hides, flax, grain and tobacco, honey.

England.—Sale of grain, butter, eggs, poultry, flax, furs, bristles, casings, fruit, and honey; purchase of metals, threshing machines, seeds, saws, minor agricul-

[1] Including Vsekoles.

as well as a considerable decrease in the export of many classes of goods (such as furs) from the Soviet Union. The turnover in the sale of different articles is shown as follows:

	1925.		1926.		1927.		1927/28.	
	£	Per Cent.	£	Per Cent.	£	Per Cent.	£	Per Cent.
Butter	100,025	64·4	1,913,891	65·7	2,282,630	74·7	2,271,151	71·0
Furs	803,142	24·7	823,199	28·3	345,841	11·3	296,992	9·3
Eggs	185,006	5·7	61,104	2·1	231,158	7·6	323,094	10·1
Poultry	62,910	1·9	50,353	1·7	92,817	3·0	161,609	5·1
Resin products	49,257	1·5	27,325	0·9	44,179	1·4	} 143,857	4·5
Various:	57,798	1·8	38,850	1·3	59,451	2·0		
Total	3,258,238	100·0	2,914,724	100·0	3,056,113	100·0	3,196,703	100·0

As may be seen from this table, the turnover in butter takes first place amongst the other exported goods, and reached the following percentages of the total: 1925, 64·6 per cent., and 1927/28, 71·0 per cent. The turnover in eggs takes second place: 1925, 5·7 per cent., and 1927/28, 10·1 per cent.; and this trade was rapidly increasing in 1927/28. The decrease in the sale of furs is due to the increase of furs sales in Germany (Leipzig). The turnover in purchases are, as noted above, much smaller than the sales, and in 1925 reached £70,734; in 1926, £79,164; in 1927, £81,371; and in 1927/28, £134,000. Amongst the goods imported from England must be noted the purchase of combined threshing machines, metals, seeds and binder twine. The smaller development in purchase is partly due to the unsatisfactory credit which English firms, as compared with other foreign firms, are in a position to give. The sale of exported goods is carried on by the London agency either independently from their own offices or through the English consumers co-operatives and through firms of brokers. The sales direct from the offices of Selosojus have greatly increased in the last few years. During these years sales have been as follows:

	1926.	1927.
Through brokers	2,946,000	2,499,000
From the office of Selosojus ..	262,000	637,000

In the year 1927, 26 per cent. of the total turnover in exported articles was sold direct.

Selosojus has branches in Hull and Glasgow, the chief purpose of which is the egg trade.

THE NEW YORK AGENCY: SELSKOSOJUS INC., NEW YORK.

The New York Agency was founded in 1924 as an American company. In the first year of its existence American firms were made acquainted with the work and requirements of the Soviet agricultural co-operatives and with their purchasing programme of agricultural machinery and appliances. Further, the credit which would be required on entering into arrangements was stated. In 1924 the Selskosojus Inc. made its first experimental purchase of thirty " Oil Pull " tractors with ploughs. The year 1925 is the first in which the American Agency undertook any considerable activity. The principal work carried on on the American market consists in the purchase of articles for import by the agricultural co-operatives, especially tractors and mowing machines; selling operations are only in the initial stage. The turnover of the American Agency in

1925, 1926 and 1927 may be seen from the following figures (in £):

	Total Turnover.	Sales.	Purchases.
1925	421,300	13,200	408,100
1926	313,700	119,700	194,000
1927	477,400	30,900	446,500
1927/28	993,000	24,000	969,000

The principal work of the Agency consists in purchasing on behalf of Selskosojus (Moscow) and Silsky Gospodar (Ukraine).

According to these tables, the purchases, which fell somewhat in 1926, had increased considerably in 1927-28. The purchase of tractors and accessories has a permanent character and is gradually increasing its scope. Deserving of special notice are the connections with Ford, with the International Harvester Company, Rumely, Massey Harris, and similar important world-known firms. Extended credit is making possible a further development of purchasing in America.

THE RIGA AGENCY: SELOSOJUS, LTD., RIGA.

The Riga Agency acts as a branch of the English company, Selosojus, Ltd., London, and is principally concerned with forwarding imported and exported goods passing to and from the Soviet Union. Comparatively little buying and selling is undertaken by the agency. The following goods are bought for import into the U.S.S.R.: red clover seeds, flax seed, timothy seed, Swedish clover, superphosphate and

large pedigree cattle. The following exports are sold:
butter, eggs, dead poultry. The turnover for 1924-
1927 gives the following figures:

	Total.		Exports.		Imports.	
	Pounds.	Per Cent.	Pounds.	Per Cent.	Pounds.	Per Cent.
1924	1,748,487	100·0	1,657,035	94·8	91,452	5·2
1925	1,254,602	71·8	1,088,026	86·7	166,576	13·3
1926	1,658,287	94·9	1,481,904	89·4	176,383	10·6
1927	1,225,053	70·1	1,079,625	88·1	145,428	11·9

The direct sales and purchase as compared with the
total turnover, are as follows:

	Total.				Purchases.				Sales.			
	Direct Trade.		Agency Business.		Direct.		Agency.		Direct.		Agency.	
	£	Per Cent.	£	Per Cent.	£	Per Cent.	£	Per Cent.	£	Per Cent.	£	Per Cent.
1924	394,697	22·6	1,353,790	77·4	63,441	69·4	28,010	30·6	331,256	20·0	1,325,780	80·0
1925	350,318	27·9	904,284	72·1	86,271	51·8	80,304	48·2	264,047	24·3	823,980	75·7
1926	219,758	13·3	1,438,529	86·7	92,135	52·2	84,248	47·8	127,623	8·6	1,354,281	91·4
1927	170,719	13·9	1,054,334	86·1	80,941	55·7	64,487	44·3	89,778	8·3	989,847	91·7

THE PARIS AGENCY: SELOSOJUS, LTD., PARIS.

The Paris agency which, like that of Riga, acts as
a branch of the English company, Selosojus, Ltd.,
London, has not yet developed its trade fully. The
turnover has been as follows: 1925, £37,383; 1926,
£33,215; and 1927, £74,000. Since 1927 the French
market began to take an interest in a few exported

articles from the Soviet Union, and it may be assumed that the sales of the Paris agency will be principally in furs, eggs and poultry. The purchase requirements depend in great part on the power of French industry to meet the needs of agriculture in the Union and on the credit provision of French firms and banks. The Paris agency has occupied itself very profitably since 1927 with the sale of flax. With the foundation of a special flax syndicate the latter has since 1927 taken over the functions of the Paris branch of Lnocentr.

FOREIGN CREDIT.

The foreign trade of the agricultural co-operatives is promoted to a large extent by the credit provided by foreign co-operatives, firms and banks. The terms and form of the credit given, which in some countries extends to five years, are extraordinarily various and depend on the business connections with individual firms and bankers in the different countries. The scope and form of credit allowed in European countries in the last three years may be seen from the following table:

	1925.		1926.		1927.	
	Pounds.	Per Cent.	Pounds.	Per Cent.	Pounds.	Per Cent.
Bank credits ..	2,858,512	64·9	2,308,813	52·2	2,490,728	45·5
Advances and credits against bills ..	1,158,204	26·3	1,415,223	32·0	1,824,472	33·4
Trading credits ..	385,992	8·8	702,336	15·8	4,154.000	21·1
Total ..	4,402,708	100·0	4,426,372	100·0	5,469,200	100·0

AGRICULTURAL CO-OPERATION

From the above table may be traced a growth in credit in the form of advances against bills made to the agricultural co-operatives. This amounted in 1925 to 26·3 per cent. of the total, and in 1927 to 33·4 per cent.; at the same time, trading credit also rose from 8·8 per cent. in 1925 to 21·1 per cent. in 1927. On the other hand, bank credits have fallen from 64·7 per cent. in 1925 to 45·5 per cent. in 1927. All credits taken together have risen 24·2 per cent. in the last two years, of which the greatest increase is that of 199 per cent. in the trading credits, while the advances have risen 57·6 per cent. and the bank credits have fallen 12·9 per cent. The greater part of the credit for exports (butter, furs, etc.) is still provided by English firms, but latterly German firms have also granted the agricultural co-operatives higher credit. In the development of credit, the credit offered by the German market especially deserves attention. In 1927 this credit had increased 113·2 per cent. compared with that of 1925, while English credits for the same period had only increased 19·4 per cent.

The acceptances of the central unions and the foreign agencies are discounted by first class foreign banks. The financing of exports usually takes the form of advances of from 20 to 40 per cent. of the value of the goods against drafts of the exporting central unions accepted by the foreign agency. Credits to from 85 to 90 per cent. of the market value of the goods to be exported are made payable at the place of consignment with deduction of the sum already advanced for exported goods. The financing of purchases takes place through foreign firms with the support of the foreign banks.

The favourable terms of credit which the agricultural co-operatives have throughout received can be attributed not only to the immaculate punctiliousness with which the agricultural co-operatives in the post-Revolution period fulfilled all their obligations, but also to the fact that they took over fully and completely the foreign obligations of the agricultural co-operatives before the revolution. The Banks affiliated to the Soviet co-operatives working abroad, and especially the Moscow Narodny Bank, Ltd., London, with its branches in Paris and Berlin and its agency in New York, and the Riga Transit Bank, are of great importance in the financing of foreign trade.

The Central Union of the agricultural co-operatives which with the Centrosojus are the principal shareholders in the Moscow Narodny Bank, contribute to the support of this Bank through their import and export operations. The balance of the Moscow Narodny Bank stood at £5,589,674 on January 1, 1928, with a balanced share capital of £1,000,000. Consequently, the Bank is in a position to put large credit in any form at the disposal of the agricultural co-operatives.

The Link with Western European Co-operatives.

The agricultural co-operative movement of the Soviet Union in its efforts to dispense as far as possible with private capital aims at establishing active business relations with Western European agricultural and consumers organisations. The scope and development of such joint operations depend, however, on practical conditions, and are in conformity with commercial objects. The direct mutual supply of the Soviet and Western European co-operatives has so

87

far only developed to an inconsiderable degree, and the trade relations with foreign co-operatives has thus by no means reached the development to be desired.

An important business connection has at present only been established with the English consumers co-operatives, particularly with the English Co-operative Wholesale Society, which on the one hand is an important consumer of butter exported through Maslocentr, and on the other is a selling and financing agency for the purchases of the agricultural co-operatives. The Co-operative Wholesale Society financed the export of 50,000 barrels of butter from the U.S.S.R. in 1926, and 100,000 barrels in 1927 and in 1928. Since 1926 the agricultural co-operatives cover a part of their purchases with this society on credit terms. The total turnover with the English Co-operative Wholesale Society in 1928 reached almost £1,000,000, counting both trade and financial transactions.

The last two years have also seen business connections with the co-operatives of other countries. Thus, the Central Union of the Latvian co-operatives, " Konsums," supplied clover seeds in the year 1926 to the value of about £26,000, and the co-operative " Association of New Owners " to the value of £7,000. Thus, about 40 per cent. of the total clover seed imported from Latvia was supplied by the co-operatives, which in 1927 amounted to £19,000, in 1927/28 to £20,000. Seeds are brought from the Czechoslovakian co-operatives, and stud horses and breeding hens from those of Sweden. Business intercourse with the German co-operative societies in spite of the obvious mutual advantages, has not yet fully developed. The turnover in butter stood at 7,000 barrels in 1927 and 18,000 in 1928. In 1928 the sale of eggs to German consumers societies also began, and amounted to twenty-five trucks. The total turnover with the German co-operative organisations in 1928 comes to more than £100,000.

Although the connection between the agricultural co-operatives of the Soviet Union and foreign co-operatives, with the exception of the English, has not so far attained any important development, there are still signs that relations will be confirmed and expanded with every year, and that the foreign co-operatives will come forward as important consumers of the exported products of the Soviet Union. It should not remain unnoticed that the interest taken in agricultural co-operation by the recent foreign co-operatives delegation during their visit to Russia, may be regarded as a sign of future development in trading relations.

The agricultural co-operatives are affiliated through their "Union of Unions" and "Silsky Gospodar" (Ukraine) to the International Co-operative Alliance (London) and the Presidents of the Union of Unions and of the Silsky Gospodar are members of the Central Committee of the Alliance. The "Union of Unions" strives through its membership of the International Co-operative Alliance to bring about a business collaboration between the agricultural co-operatives of the Soviet Union and the Co-operatives of Western Europe. The earnest attention which the International Co-operative Alliance gives to the question of relations between agricultural and consumers co-operative societies, the discussion of this question at the International Co-operative Congress at Stockholm in August, 1927, and at the meeting of the Central Committee of the Alliance in Geneva in November, 1928, gives every reason for thinking that further trade between the two chief branches of the co-operative movement (industrial and agricultural) has great possibilities of future development. The practical experience of the Agricultural Co-operatives of the U.S.S.R., which have already established considerable undertakings on these lines, prove that nothing but mutual advantage can be gained from such relations.

For Product Safety Concerns and Information please contact our EU
representative GPSR@taylorandfrancis.com
Taylor & Francis Verlag GmbH, Kaufingerstraße 24, 80331 München, Germany

www.ingramcontent.com/pod-product-compliance
Ingram Content Group UK Ltd.
Pitfield, Milton Keynes, MK11 3LW, UK
UKHW021825240425
457818UK00006B/80